TABLE OF CONTENTS

SEXUAL PRIVACY
61

"Would we allow the police to search the sacred precincts of the marital bedrooms for telltale signs of the use of contraceptives? The very idea is repulsive to the notions of privacy surrounding the marriage relationship."

Justice William Douglas
Griswold v. Connecticut (1965)

CENSORSHIP
69

". . . when everything is classified, then nothing is classified, and the system becomes one to be disregarded by the cynical or the careless, and to be manipulated by those intent on self-protection or self-promotion." - The Pentagon Papers Case.

Justice Potter Stewart
New York Times v. United States (1971)

ABORTION
89

"One's philosophy, one's experiences, one's exposure to the raw edges of human existence, one's religious training, one's attitudes toward life and family and their values, and the moral standards one establishes and seeks to observe, are all likely to influence and to color one's thinking and conclusions about abortion."

Justice Harry Blackmun
Roe v. Wade (1973)

". . . the Court's opinion will accomplish the seemingly impossible feat of leaving this area of the law more confused than it found it."

Justice William Rehnquist, dissenting
Roe v. Wade (1973)

AFFIRMATIVE ACTION
127

"The guarantee of equal protection cannot mean one thing when applied to one individual and something else when applied to a person of another color. If both are not accorded the same protection, then it is not equal."

Justice Lewis Powell
University of California v. Bakke (1978)

LANDMARK DECISIONS OF THE UNITED STATES SUPREME COURT

MAUREEN HARRISON & STEVE GILBERT
EDITORS

LANDMARK DECISIONS SERIES

EXCELLENT BOOKS
BEVERLY HILLS, CALIFORNIA

EXCELLENT BOOKS
Post Office Box 7121
Beverly Hills, CA 90212-712

Copyright © 1991 by Excellent Books.

"This publication is designed to provide accurate and authoritative information in regard to the subject matter covered. It is sold with the understanding that the publisher is not engaged in rendering legal or other professional service. If legal advice or other expert assistance is required, the services of a competent professional person should be sought." - From a Declaration of Principles jointly adopted by a Committee of the American Bar Association and a Committee of Publishers.

Publisher's Cataloging in Publication Data

Landmark Decisions Of The United States Supreme Court /
 Maureen Harrison, Steve Gilbert, editors.
 p. cm. - (Landmark Decisions Series)
Bibliography: p.
Includes Index.
1. United States. Supreme Court.
I. Title. II. Harrison, Maureen. III. Gilbert, Steve.
IV. Series: Landmark Decisions.
KF8742.H24 1991   LC 90-084578
347.'73'26-dc20
[347.30726]
ISBN 0-9628014-1-0
ISBN 0-9628014-0-2 (Landmark Decisions Series)

Note To The Reader . . .

The Supreme Court of the United States is the Court of Final Appeal for all legal controversies in the federal courts and all federal issues arising in the state courts. Only the Court has the authority to construct and interpret the meaning of the Constitution. "We are not final," wrote Justice Robert Jackson, "because we are infallible, but we are infallible because we are final."

Appeals to the Court for a final determination come from all over the country on a wide spectrum of controversies. Some cases have begun years earlier, going through their state's system of trial, intermediate and final appeals courts. Others originate in the federal trial courts and are appealed first to an intermediate appeals court and then to the Supreme Court. Still others are heard only by the Court itself.

The Justices review only about 150 cases a year, and four of the nine Justices must agree to that review. Written arguments [briefs] are submitted and oral arguments are heard. Soon after, the nine Justices meet in Conference to vote on whether they will affirm, remand or reverse, in whole or in part, the decisions of the lower courts from which these appeals have come. In rare instances the Court will issue its decision *per curiam* [by the court], speaking with one voice without attribution of authorship. Usually, it is one Justice, voting in the majority, who will be selected to write the majority opinion. Others may join in the majority opinion, write their own concurring opinion, write their own dissenting opinion, or join in another's concurrence or dissent. Drafts of the majority, concurring, and dissenting opinions circulate among the Justices, are redrafted, and recirculated, until a consensus, months or even years later, is finally reached and a decision announced. It is the majority opinion as finally issued by the Court that stands as the law of the land.

The Court has issued thousands of decisions. All have been important to the parties involved, but some, a significant few, have grown so important as to involve us all. These are Landmark Decisions, fundamentally altering the relationships of Americans to their institutions and to each other. Of these significant few the editors have selected ten for inclusion in this book. The decisions, issued between 1954 and 1989 by the Warren-Berger-Rehnquist Courts represent the great and continuing controversies of our times and are presented here for the first time to the general reader.

These ten Landmark Decisions are carefully edited versions of the official texts issued by the Supreme Court in United States Reports. The editors have made every effort to put reading ease into legalese without damaging the original decisions. Edited out are long legal citations, micro print footnotes, and wordy wrangles over points of procedure. Edited in [in brackets] are definitions [*writ of habeas corpus* = an order from a judge to bring a person to court], translations [*certiorari* = the decision of the Court to review a case], identifications [Appellant = Roe, Appellee = Wade], and explanations [where the case originated, how it got to the court, and who the parties were] You will find in this book the majority opinion of the Court as expressed by the Justice chosen to speak for the Court. Concurring and dissenting opinions, with a few notable exceptions, have not been included. At the beginning of each edited decision we note where the entire decision can be found, and in the bibliography we provide a list of further reading. Also included is a list of Justices participating in these decisions and, for the reader's reference, a complete copy of the U.S. Constitution, to which every decision refers.

v. is the legal abbreviation for 'versus.' The name of the person or group appealing a lower court decision goes to the left of the v. the person or group defending goes to the right. Before there can be an appeal, there must be a trial. State trial courts (Municipal, County, Superior or Circuit Courts) and Federal trial courts (U.S. District Courts) examine facts and issues. State appeal courts (Court of Appeals, Appellate Divisions, Appellate Courts) and Federal appeals courts (U.S. Courts of Appeals) review, for errors, the decisions of trial courts. State Supreme Courts review, for errors, the decisions of State Trial Courts. The U.S. Supreme Court, at its discreation, reviews, for errors, the decisions of the U.S. Courts of Appeals, or the U.S. District Courts, or, on federal issues, State Supreme Courts or State Appeals Courts.

In an appeal the Court will either Affirm - let the lower court decision stand, or Remand - send it back to the lower court for further work or, Reverse - change the lower court decision. The Courts reasons for Affirming or Remanding or Reversing appear in the majority opinion. Concurring opinions, in agreement with the majority or dissenting opinions, disagreeing with the majority opinion may be issued. It is the key principals majority opinion that are binding precident on all lower courts in all similar cases.

We entered into editing this book because we, like you, and your family and friends, must obey, under penalty of law, the decisions of the U.S. Supreme Court. It stands to reason that, if we owe them our obedience then we owe it to ourselves to know what they say, not second-hand, but for ourselves. We think it's time for you to be the Judge.

M.H. & S.G.

This book is dedicated to our fathers . . .

John
1922 - 1985

Sol
1915 - 1957

ABOUT THE EDITORS . . .

MAUREEN HARRISON is a textbook editor and a
member of the Supreme Court Historical Society

STEVE GILBERT is a law librarian and a member of the
American Association of Law Libraries and the American
Bar Association

The editors are currently at work on the second book in
the Landmark Decisions Series

BOOK BANNING
159

"If there is any fixed star in our constitutional constellation, it is that no official, high or petty, can prescribe, what shall be orthodox in politics, nationalism, religion, or other matters of opinion. . . . If there are any circumstances which permit an exception, they do not now occur to us."

Justice William Brennan
Board Of Education v. Pico (1982)

FLAG BURNING
175

"If there is a bedrock principle underlying the First Amendment, it is that the Government may not prohibit the expression of an idea simply because society finds the idea itself offensive or disagreeable."

Justice William Brennan
Texas v. Johnson (1989)

THE U.S. CONSTITUTION
195

"We the people of the United States, in order to form a more perfect union, establish justice, insure domestic tranquility, provide for the common defense, promote the general welfare, and secure the blessings of liberty to ourselves and our posterity, do ordain and establish this Constitution for the United States of America."

The Preamble (1789)

SCHOOL DESEGREGATION

BROWN v. BOARD OF EDUCATION

The School Desegregation Decision originates in Kansas. The decision combines four separate school desegregation cases decided together. In addition to *Brown* (Kansas), there were *Briggs* (South Carolina), *Davis* (Virginia), and *Gebhart* (Delaware).

The parents of Linda Brown, a young black schoolgirl attending a segregated elementary school in Topeka, sued in U.S. District Court on her behalf the members of the Board of Education, trying to stop them from enforcing a Kansas law that permitted, but did not require, cities like Topeka to maintain separate school facilities for white and black children.

The District Court refused to admit Linda Brown to an all-white school based on an 1896 U.S. Supreme Court decision. An appeal was made to the Supreme Court which agreed to a review.

Oral arguments were presented to the Court on December 9, 1952, the case was reargued on December 8, 1953 and was decided on May 17, 1954.

The unanimous decision of the court was delivered by Chief Justice Earl Warren.

The full text of *Brown v. Board of Education* can be found in United States Reports, volume 347, on page 483.

BROWN v. BOARD OF EDUCATION

May 17, 1954

CHIEF JUSTICE EARL WARREN: These cases come to us from the States of Kansas, South Carolina, Virginia, and Delaware. They are premised on different facts and different local conditions, but a common legal question justifies their consideration together in this consolidated opinion.

In each of the cases, minors of the Negro race [called the plaintiffs], through their legal representatives, seek the aid of the courts in obtaining admission to the public schools of their community on a nonsegregated basis. In each instance, they had been denied admission to schools attended by white children under laws requiring or permitting segregation according to race. This segregation was alleged to deprive the plaintiffs of the equal protection of the laws under the Fourteenth Amendment. In each of the cases other than the Delaware case, a three-judge federal district court denied relief to the plaintiffs on the so-called "separate but equal" doctrine announced by this Court in [the 1896 decision] *Plessy v. Ferguson.* Under that doctrine, equality of treatment is accorded when the races are provided substantially equal facilities, even though these facilities be separate. In the Delaware case, the Supreme Court of Delaware adhered to that doctrine, but ordered that the plaintiffs be admitted to the white schools because of their superiority to the Negro schools.

The plaintiffs contend that segregated public schools are not "equal" and cannot be made "equal," and that hence they are deprived of the equal protection of the laws. Be-

cause of the obvious importance of the question presented, the Court [agreed to hear the case]. Argument was
heard in the 1952 Term, and reargument was heard this
Term on certain questions [asked] by the Court.

Reargument was largely devoted to the circumstances surrounding the adoption of the Fourteenth Amendment in
1868. It covered exhaustively consideration of the
Amendment in Congress, ratification by the states, then
existing practices in racial segregation, and the views of
proponents and opponents of the Amendment. This discussion and our own investigation convince us that, although these sources cast some light, it is not enough to
resolve the problem with which we are faced. At best,
they are inconclusive. The most avid proponents of the
post-[Civil] War Amendments undoubtedly intended them
to remove all legal distinctions among "all persons born or
naturalized in the United States." Their opponents, just as
certainly, were antagonistic to both the letter and the spirit of the Amendments and wished them to have the most
limited effect. What others in Congress and the state legislatures had in mind cannot be determined with any degree of certainty.

An additional reason for the inconclusive nature of the
Amendment's history, with respect to segregated schools,
is the status of public education at that time. In the
South, the movement toward free common schools, supported by general taxation, had not yet taken hold. Education of white children was largely in the hands of private groups. Education of Negroes was almost non-
existent, and practically all of the race were illiterate. In
fact, any education of Negroes was forbidden by law in
some states. Today, in contrast, many Negroes have
achieved outstanding success in the arts and sciences as

well as in the business and professional world. It is true
that public school education at the time of the Amendment had advanced further in the North, but the effect of
the Amendment on Northern States was generally ignored
in the Congressional debates. Even in the North, the conditions of public education did not approximate those existing today. The curriculum was usually rudimentary;
ungraded schools were common in rural areas; the school
term was but three months a year in many states; and
compulsory school attendance was virtually unknown. As
a consequence, it is not surprising that there should be so
little in the history of the Fourteenth Amendment relating to its intended effect on public education.

In the first cases in this Court construing the Fourteenth
Amendment, decided shortly after its adoption, the Court
interpreted it as [prohibiting] all state-imposed discrimi-
nations against the Negro race. The doctrine of "separate
but equal" did not make its appearance in this Court until
1896 in the case of *Plessy v. Ferguson*, involving not education but transportation. American courts have since la-
bored with the doctrine for over half a century. In this
Court, there have been six cases involving the "separate
but equal" doctrine in the field of public education. In
Cumming v. County Board of Education, and *Gong Lum
v. Rice*, the validity of the doctrine itself was not challenged. In more recent cases, all on the graduate school
level, inequality was found in that specific benefits enjoyed by white students were denied to Negro students of
the same educational qualifications. In none of these
cases was it necessary to re-examine the doctrine to grant
relief to the Negro plaintiff. And in *Sweatt v. Painter*,
the Court expressly reserved decision on the question
whether *Plessy v. Ferguson* should be held inapplicable to
public education.

In [these] cases, that question is directly presented. Here, unlike *Sweatt v. Painter*, there are findings [in lower State and Federal Courts] that the Negro and white schools involved have been equalized, or are being equalized, with respect to buildings, curricula, qualifications and salaries of teachers, and other "tangible" factors. Our decision, therefore, cannot turn on merely a comparison of these tangible factors in the Negro and white schools involved in each of the cases. We must look instead to the effect of segregation itself on public education.

In approaching this problem, we cannot turn the clock back to 1868 when the Amendment was adopted, or even to 1896 when *Plessy v. Ferguson* was written.

We must consider public education in the light of its full development and its present place in American life throughout the Nation. Only in this way can it be determined if segregation in public schools deprives these plaintiffs of the equal protection of the laws.

Today, education is perhaps the most important function of state and local governments. Compulsory school attendance laws and the great expenditures for education both demonstrate our recognition of the importance of education to our democratic society. It is required in the performance of our most basic public responsibilities, even service in the armed forces. It is the very foundation of good citizenship. Today it is a principal instrument in awakening the child to cultural values, in preparing him for later professional training, and in helping him to adjust normally to his environment. In these days, it is doubtful that any child may reasonably be expected to succeed in life if he is denied the opportunity of an education. Such an opportunity, where the state has undertaken to provide it, is a right which must be made available to all on equal terms.

We come then to the question presented: Does segregation of children in public schools solely on the basis of race, even though the physical facilities and other "tangible" factors may be equal, deprive the children of the minority group of equal educational opportunities? We believe that it does.

In *Sweatt v. Painter*, in finding that a segregated law school for Negroes could not provide them equal educational opportunities, this Court relied in large part on "those qualities which are incapable of objective measurement but which make for greatness in a law school." In *McLaurin v. Oklahoma State Regents*, the Court, in requiring that a Negro admitted to a white graduate school be treated like all other students, again resorted to intangible considerations: ". . . his ability to study, to engage in discussions and exchange views with other students, and, in general, to learn his profession." Such considerations apply with added force to children in grade and high schools. To separate them from others of similar age and qualifications solely because of their race generates a feeling of inferiority as to their status in the community that may affect their hearts and minds in a way unlikely ever to be undone. The effect of this separation on their educational opportunities was well stated by a finding in the Kansas case by a court which nevertheless felt compelled to rule against the Negro plaintiffs:

"Segregation of white and colored children in public schools has a detrimental effect upon the colored children. The impact is greater when it has the sanction of the law; for the policy of separating the races is usually interpreted as denoting the inferiority of the negro group. A sense of inferiority affects the motivation of a child to learn. Segregation with the sanction of law, therefore, has a tendency to [retard] the educational and mental development of negro children and to deprive them of some of the benefits they would receive in a racial[ly] integrated school system."

Whatever may have been the extent of psychological knowledge at the time of *Plessy v. Ferguson*, this finding is amply supported by modern authority. Any language in *Plessy v. Ferguson* contrary to this finding is rejected.

We conclude that in the field of public education the doctrine of "separate but equal" has no place. Separate educational facilities are inherently unequal. Therefore, we hold that the plaintiffs and others similarly situated for whom the actions have been brought are, by reason of the segregation complained of, deprived of the equal protection of the laws guaranteed by the Fourteenth Amendment. This disposition makes unnecessary any discussion whether such segregation also violates the Due Process Clause of the Fourteenth Amendment.

Because these are class actions [where one person represents a larger group], because of the wide applicability of this decision, and because of the great variety of local conditions, the formulation of decrees [orders of the court] in these cases presents problems of considerable complexity. On reargument, the consideration of appropriate relief [how to end school segregation] was necessarily subordinated to the primary question - the constitutionality of segregation in public education. We have now announced that such segregation is a denial of the equal protection of the laws. In order that we may have the full assistance of the parties in formulating decrees, the cases will be restored to the docket [put on the Court's calendar], and the parties are requested to present further argument on [these issues] for the reargument this Term. The Attorney General of the United States is again invited to participate. The Attorneys General of the states requiring or permitting segregation in public education will also be permitted to appear as *amici curiae* [friends of the Court] upon request to do so by September 15, 1954, and submission of briefs by October 1, 1954.

It is so ordered.

[In 1955 in the *Brown II* decision, the Court ordered that U.S. public schools be desegregated with "all deliberate speed."]

OBSCENITY

ROTH v. UNITED STATES

The Obscenity Decision originates in New York and California. Two separate obscenity cases *Roth* (New York) and *Alberts* (California) were decided together.

Roth was found guilty in a U.S. District Court of violations of the obscenity provisions of the United States Code. Roth's conviction was affirmed by the U.S. Court of Appeals. Roth appealed his conviction and the U.S. Supreme Court granted a review.

Alberts was found guilty in Beverly Hills Municipal Court of violations of the obscenity provisions of the California Code. Alberts' conviction was affirmed by the Appellate Department of the Superior Court of the State of California in and for the County of Los Angeles. Alberts appealed his conviction and the U.S. Supreme Court granted a review.

Oral arguments were heard April 3, 1962 and a decision was announced June 25, 1962.

The decision of the Court was delivered by Justice William Brennan. Chief Justice Earl Warren concurred. Justice John Marshall Harlan concurred in part and dissented in part. Justices William Douglas and Hugo Black dissented.

The full text of *Roth v. United States* can be found in United States Reports, volume 354, page 476.

ROTH v. UNITED STATES

June 24, 1957

JUSTICE WILLIAM BRENNAN: The constitutionality of a criminal obscenity statute is the question in each of these cases. In *Roth*, the primary constitutional question is whether the federal obscenity statute violates the provision of the First Amendment that "Congress shall make no law ... abridging the freedom of speech, or of the press ... ." In *Alberts*, the primary constitutional question is whether the obscenity provisions of the California Penal Code invade the freedoms of speech and press as they may be incorporated in the liberty protected from state action by the Due Process Clause of the Fourteenth Amendment.

Other constitutional questions are: whether these statutes violate due process, because too vague to support conviction for crime; whether power to punish speech and press offensive to decency and morality is in the States alone, so that the federal obscenity statute violates the Ninth and Tenth Amendments (raised in *Roth*); and whether Congress, by enacting the federal obscenity statute, ... to establish post offices and post roads, pre-empted the regulation of the subject matter (raised in *Alberts*).

Roth conducted a business in New York in the publication and sale of books, photographs and magazines. He used circulars and advertising matter to solicit sales. He was convicted by a jury in the District Court for the Southern District of New York upon 4 counts of a 26-count indictment charging him with mailing obscene circulars and advertising, and an obscene book, in violation of the federal obscenity statute. His conviction was affirmed [upheld] by the Court of Appeals for the Second Circuit. We granted certiorari [agreed to review this case].

Alberts conducted a mail-order business from Los Angeles. He was convicted by the Judge of the Municipal Court of the Beverly Hills Judicial District (having waived a jury trial) under a misdemeanor complaint which charged him with lewdly keeping for sale obscene and indecent books, and with writing, composing and publishing an obscene advertisement of them, in violation of the California Penal Code. The conviction was affirmed by the Appellate Department of the Superior Court of the State of California in and for the County of Los Angeles.

The . . . question is whether obscenity is utterance within the area of protected speech and press. Although this is the first time the question has been squarely presented to this Court, either under the First Amendment or under the Fourteenth Amendment, expressions found in numerous opinions indicate that this Court has always assumed that obscenity is not protected by the freedoms of speech and press. . . .

The guaranties of freedom of expression in effect in 10 [Delaware, Georgia, Maryland, Massachusetts, New Hampshire, North Carolina, Pennsylvania, South Carolina, Vermont, and Virginia) of the 14 States which by 1792 had ratified the Constitution, gave no absolute protection for every utterance. Thirteen of the 14 States provided for the prosecution of libel, and all of those States made either blasphemy or profanity, or both, statutory crimes. As early as 1712, Massachusetts made it criminal to publish "any filthy, obscene, or profane song, pamphlet, libel or-mock sermon" in imitation or mimicking of religious services. Thus, profanity and obscenity were related offenses.

In light of this history, it is apparent that the unconditional phrasing of the First Amendment was not intended to protect every utterance. This phrasing did not prevent this Court from concluding that libelous utterances are not within the area of constitutionally protected speech. At the time of the adoption of the First Amendment, obscenity law was not as fully developed as libel law, but there is sufficient . . . evidence to show that obscenity, too, was outside the protection intended for speech and press.

The protection given speech and press was fashioned to assure unfettered interchange of ideas for the bringing about of political and social changes desired by the people. This objective was made explicit as early as 1774 in a letter of the Continental Congress to the inhabitants of Quebec:

> "The last right we shall mention, regards the freedom of the press. The importance of this consists, besides the advancement of truth, science, morality, and arts in general, in its diffusion of liberal sentiments on the administration of Government, its ready communication of thoughts between subjects, and its consequential promotion of union among them, whereby oppressive officers are shamed or intimidated, into more honourable and just modes of conducting affairs."

All ideas having even the slightest redeeming social importance - unorthodox ideas, controversial ideas, even ideas hateful to the prevailing climate of opinion - have the full protection of the guaranties, unless excludable because they encroach upon the limited area of more impor-

tant interests. But implicit in the history of the First
Amendment is the rejection of obscenity as utterly without redeeming social importance. This rejection for that
reason is mirrored in the universal judgment that obscenity should be restrained, reflected in [an] international
agreement of over 50 nations, in the obscenity laws of all
of the 48 States, and in the 20 obscenity laws enacted by
the Congress from 1842 to 1956. This is the same judgment expressed by this Court in *Chaplinsky v. New
Hampshire*:

> "... There are certain well-defined and nar-
> rowly limited classes of speech, the preven-
> tion and punishment of which have never
> been thought to raise any Constitutional
> problem. *These include the lewd and ob-
> scene . . . . It has been well observed that
> such utterances are no essential part of any
> exposition of ideas, and are of such slight
> social value as a step to truth that any bene-
> fit that may be derived from them is clearly
> outweighed by the social interest in order
> and morality. . . .*"

We hold that obscenity is not within the area of constitutionally protected speech or press.

It is strenuously urged that these obscenity statutes offend
the constitutional guaranties because they punish incita-
tion to impure sexual *thoughts,* not shown to be related to
any overt antisocial conduct which is or may be incited in
the persons stimulated to such *thoughts.* In *Roth,* the trial
judge instructed the jury: "The words 'obscene, lewd and
lascivious' as used in the law, signify that form of immor-
ality which has relation to sexual impurity and has a tend-

ency to excite lustful *thoughts*." In *Alberts*, the trial
judge applied the test laid down in *People v. Wepplo*,
namely, whether the material has a "substantial tendency
to deprave or corrupt its readers by inciting lascivious
thoughts or arousing lustful desires." It is insisted that the
constitutional guaranties are violated because convictions
may be had without proof either that obscene material
will perceptibly create a clear and present danger of antisocial conduct, or will probably induce its recipients to
such conduct. But, in light of our holding that obscenity
is not protected speech, the complete answer to this argument is in the holding of this Court in *Beauharnais v. Illi-
nois*.

> "Libelous utterances not being within the
> area of constitutionally protected speech, it
> is unnecessary, either for us or for the State
> courts, to consider the issues behind the
> phrase 'clear and present danger.' Certainly
> no one would contend that obscene speech,
> for example, may be punished only upon a
> showing of such circumstances. Libel, as
> we have seen, is in the same class."

However, sex and obscenity are not synonymous. Obscene
material is material which deals with sex in a manner appealing to prurient interest. The portrayal of sex, *e.g.*, in
art, literature and scientific works, is not itself sufficient
reason to deny material the constitutional protection of
freedom of speech and press. Sex, a great and mysterious
motive force in human life, has indisputably been a subject of absorbing interest to mankind through the ages; it
is one of the vital problems of human interest and public
concern. As to all such problems, this Court said in
Thornhill v. Alabama.

"The freedom of speech and of the press guaranteed by the Constitution embraces at the least the liberty to discuss publicly and truthfully *all matters of public concern* without previous restraint or fear of subsequent punishment. The exigencies of the colonial period and the efforts to secure freedom from oppressive administration developed a broadened conception of these liberties as adequate to supply the public need for *information and education with respect to the significant issues of the times.* . . . Freedom of discussion, if it would fulfill its historic function in this nation, must embrace *all issues about which information is needed or appropriate to enable the members of society to cope with the exigencies of their period."*

The fundamental freedoms of speech and press have contributed greatly to the development and well-being of our free society and are indispensable to its continued growth. Ceaseless vigilance is the watchword to prevent their erosion by Congress or by the States. The door barring federal and state intrusion into this area cannot be left ajar; it must be kept tightly closed and opened only the slightest crack necessary to prevent encroachment upon more important interests. It is therefore vital that the standards for judging obscenity safeguard the protection of freedom of speech and press for material which does not treat sex in a manner appealing to prurient interest.

The early leading standard of obscenity allowed material to be judged merely by the effect of an isolated excerpt upon particularly susceptible persons. Some American courts adopted this standard but later decisions have rejected it and substituted this test: whether to the average person, applying contemporary community standards, the dominant theme of the material taken as a whole appeals to prurient interest. The *Hicklin* test, judging obscenity by the effect of isolated passages upon the most susceptible persons, might well encompass material legitimately treating with sex, and so it must be rejected as unconstitutionally restrictive of the freedoms of speech and press. On the other hand, the substituted standard provides safeguards adequate to withstand the charge of constitutional infirmity.

Both trial courts below sufficiently followed the proper standard. Both courts used the proper definition of obscenity. In addition, in the *Alberts* case, . . . the trial judge indicated that, as the trier of facts, he was judging each item as a whole as it would affect the normal person, and in *Roth*, the trial judge instructed the jury as follows:

> ". . . The test is not whether it would arouse sexual desires or sexual impure thoughts in those comprising a particular segment of the community, the young, the immature or the highly prudish or would leave another segment, the scientific or highly educated or the so-called worldly-wise and sophisticated indifferent and unmoved. . . .

> "The test in each case is the effect of the book, picture or publication considered as a whole, not upon any particular class, but upon all those whom it is likely to reach. In other words, you determine its impact upon the average person in the community.

The books, pictures and circulars must be
judged as a whole, in their entire context,
and you are not to consider detached or
separate portions in reaching a conclusion.
You judge the circulars, pictures and publi-
cations which have been put in evidence by
present-day standards of the community.
You may ask yourselves does it offend the
common conscience of the community by
present-day standards.

"In this case, ladies and gentlemen of the
jury, you and you alone are the exclusive
judges of what the common conscience of
the community is, and in determining that
conscience you are to consider the community as a whole, young and old, educated
and uneducated, the religious and the irreli-
gious - men, women and children."

It is argued that the statutes do not provide reasonably as-
certainable standards of guilt and therefore violate the
constitutional requirements of due process. The federal
obscenity statute makes punishable the mailing of material that is "obscene, lewd, lascivious, or filthy . . . or other
publication of an indecent character." The California statute makes punishable, *[among other things]*, the keeping
for sale or advertising material that is "obscene or indecent." The thrust of the argument is that these words are
not sufficiently precise because they do not mean the
same thing to all people, all the time, everywhere.

Many decisions have recognized that these terms of obscenity statutes are not precise. This Court, however, has
consistently held that lack of precision is not itself offen-

sive to the requirements of due process. ". . . [T]he Constitution does not require impossible standards"; all that is required is that the language "conveys sufficiently definite warning as to the proscribed [prohibited] conduct when measured by common understanding and practices." These words, applied according to the proper standard for judging obscenity, already discussed, give adequate warning of the conduct proscribed and mark ". . . boundaries sufficiently distinct for judges and juries fairly to administer the law. . . . That there may be marginal cases in which it is difficult to determine the side of the line on which a particular fact situation falls is no sufficient reason to hold the language too ambiguous to define a criminal offense. . . ."

In summary, then, we hold that these statutes, applied according to the proper standard for judging obscenity, do not offend constitutional safeguards against convictions based upon protected material, or fail to give men in acting adequate notice of what is prohibited.

Roth's argument that the federal obscenity statute unconstitutionally encroaches upon the powers reserved by the Ninth and Tenth Amendments to the States and to the people to punish speech and press where offensive to decency and morality is hinged upon his contention that obscenity is expression not excepted from the sweep of the provision of the First Amendment that "*Congress* shall make *no law* . . . abridging the freedom of speech, or of the press. . . ." That argument falls in light of our holding that obscenity is not expression protected by the First Amendment. We therefore hold that the federal obscenity statute punishing the use of the mails for obscene material is a proper exercise of the postal power delegated to Congress by Art. I, [Section] 8, cl. 7.

Alberts argues that because his was a mail-order business, the California statute is repugnant to Art. I, [Section] 8, cl. 7, under which the Congress allegedly pre-empted the regulatory field by enacting the federal obscenity statute punishing the mailing or advertising by mail of obscene material. The federal statute deals only with actual mailing; it does not eliminate the power of the state to punish "keeping for sale" or "advertising" obscene material. The state statute in no way imposes a burden or interferes with the federal postal functions. ". . . The decided cases which indicate the limits of state regulatory power in relation to the federal mail service involve situations where state regulation involved a direct, physical interference with federal activities under the postal power or some direct, immediate burden on the performance of the postal functions. . . ."

The judgments are *affirmed.*

SCHOOL PRAYER

ENGEL v. VITALE

The School Prayer Decision originates in New York. The Board of Education of New Hyde Park directed that a prayer, provided by the New York State Board of Regents, was to be recited by the students at the beginning of each school day. Several parents, including Stephen Engel, objected and sued the State of New York and the the School Board, whose President was William Vitale, Jr.

The case was tried in a Nassau County Court and was won by the State and the School Board. The parents appealed to the Appellate Division of the New York State Supreme Court and the New York Court of Appeals. The result was the same. They then appealed to the U.S. Supreme Court, which agreed to a review.

Oral arguments were heard on April 3, 1962 and a decision was rendered on June 25.

Justice Hugo Black delivered the opinion of the Court. Justice William Douglas concurred.

Justice Potter Stewart filed a dissenting opinion. Justices Felix Frankfurter and Byron White took no part in the decision.

The full text of *Engel v. Vitale* can be found in United States Reports, volume 370, page 421.

ENGEL v. VITALE

June 25, 1962

JUSTICE HUGO BLACK: The respondent Board of Education of Union Free School District No. 9, New Hyde Park, New York, acting in its official capacity under state law, directed the School District's principal to cause the following prayer to be said aloud by each class in the presence of a teacher at the beginning of each school day:

> "Almighty God, we acknowledge our dependence upon Thee, and we beg Thy blessings upon us, our parents, our teachers and our Country."

This daily procedure was adopted on the recommendation of the State Board of Regents, a governmental agency created by the State Constitution to which the New York Legislature has granted broad supervisory, executive, and legislative powers over the State's public school system. These state officials composed the prayer which they recommended and published as a part of their "Statement on Moral and Spiritual Training in the Schools," saying: "We believe that this Statement will be subscribed to by all men and women of good will, and we call upon all of them to aid in giving life to our program."

Shortly after the practice of reciting the Regents' prayer was adopted by the School District, the parents of ten pupils brought this action in a New York State Court insisting that use of this official prayer in the public schools was contrary to the beliefs, religions, or religious practices of both themselves and their children. Among other things, these parents challenged the constitutionality of

both the state law authorizing the School District to direct
the use of prayer in public schools and the School District's regulation ordering the recitation of this particular
prayer on the ground that these actions of official governmental agencies violate that part of the First Amendment
of the Federal Constitution which commands that
"Congress shall make no law respecting an establishment
of religion" - a command which was "made applicable to
the State of New York by the Fourteenth Amendment of
the said Constitution." The New York Court of Appeals,
over the dissents of Judges Dye and Fuld, sustained [let
stand] an order of the lower state courts which had upheld the power of New York to use the Regents' prayer as
a part of the daily procedures of its public schools so long
as the schools did not compel any pupil to join in the
prayer over his or his parents' objection. We granted certiorari [agreed to] review this important decision involving rights protected by the First and Fourteenth Amendments.

We think that by using its public school system to encourage recitation of the Regents' prayer, the State of New
York has adopted a practice wholly inconsistent with the
Establishment Clause. There can, of course, be no doubt
that New York's program of daily classroom invocation of
God's blessings as prescribed in the Regents' prayer is a
religious activity. It is a solemn avowal of divine faith
and supplication for the blessings of the Almighty. The
nature of such a prayer has always been religious, none of
the [members of the School Board] has denied this and the
trial court expressly so found:

> "The religious nature of prayer was recog-
> nized by Jefferson and has been concurred
> in by theological writers, the United States

Supreme Court and State courts and administrative officials, including New York's
Commissioner of Education. A committee
of the New York Legislature has agreed.

"The Board of Regents . . . , the [School
Board] and [other interested parties] all
concede the religious nature of prayer, but
seek to distinguish this prayer because it is
based on our spiritual heritage. . . ."

The petitioners contend among other things that the state
laws requiring or permitting use of the Regents' prayer
must be struck down as a violation of the Establishment
Clause [of the Fourteenth Amendment] because that prayer was composed by governmental officials as a part of a
governmental program to further religious beliefs. For
this reason, petitioners argue, the State's use of the Regents' prayer in its public school system breaches the constitutional wall of separation between Church and State.
We agree with that contention since we think that the
constitutional prohibition against laws respecting an establishment of religion must at least mean that in this country it is no part of the business of government to compose
official prayers for any group of the American people to
recite as a part of a religious program carried on by government.

It is a matter of history that this very practice of establishing governmentally composed prayers for religious
services was one of the reasons which caused many of our
early colonists to leave England and seek religious freedom in America. The Book of Common Prayer, which
was created under governmental direction and which was
approved by Acts of Parliament in 1548 and 1549, set out

in minute detail the accepted form and content of prayer and other religious ceremonies to be used in the established, tax-supported Church of England. The controversies over the Book and what should be its content repeatedly threatened to disrupt the peace of that country as the accepted forms of prayer in the established church changed with the views of the particular ruler that happened to be in control at the time. Powerful groups representing some of the varying religious views of the people struggled among themselves to impress their particular views upon the Government and obtain amendments of the Book more suitable to their respective notions of how religious services should be conducted in order that the official religious establishment would advance their particular religious beliefs. Other groups, lacking the necessary political power to influence the Government on the matter, decided to leave England and its established church and seek freedom in America from England's governmentally ordained and supported religion.

It is an unfortunate fact of history that when some of the very groups which had most strenuously opposed the established Church of England found themselves sufficiently in control of colonial governments in this country to write their own prayers into law, they passed laws making their own religion the official religion of their respective colonies. Indeed, as late as the time of the Revolutionary War, there were established churches in at least eight of the thirteen former colonies and established religions in at least four of the other five. But the successful Revolution against English political domination was shortly followed by intense opposition to the practice of establishing religion by law. This opposition crystallized rapidly into an effective political force in Virginia where the minority religious groups such as Presbyterians, Lutherans, Quakers and Baptists had gained such strength that the adherents to the established Episcopal Church were actually a minority themselves. In 1785-1786, those opposed to the established Church, led by James Madison and Thomas Jefferson, who, though themselves not members of any of these dissenting religious groups, opposed all religious establishments by law on grounds of principle, obtained the enactment of the famous "Virginia Bill for Religious Liberty" by which all religious groups were placed on an equal footing so far as the State was concerned. Similar though less far-reaching legislation was being considered and passed in other States.

By the time of the adoption of the Constitution, our history shows that there was a widespread awareness among many Americans of the dangers of a union of Church and State. These people knew, some of them from bitter personal experience, that one of the greatest dangers to the freedom of the individual to worship in his own way lay in the Government's placing its official stamp of approval upon one particular kind of prayer or one particular form of religious services. They knew the anguish, hardship and bitter strife that could come when zealous religious groups struggled with one another to obtain the Government's stamp of approval from each King, Queen, or Protector that came to temporary power. The Constitution was intended to avert a part of this danger by leaving the government of this country in the hands of the people rather than in the hands of any monarch. But this safeguard was not enough. Our Founders were no more willing to let the content of their prayers and their privilege of praying whenever they pleased be influenced by the ballot box than they were to let these vital matters of personal conscience depend upon the succession of monarchs. The First Amendment was added to the Constitution to stand as a guarantee that neither the power nor the prestige of the Federal Government would be used to control, support or influence the kinds of prayer the American people can say - that the people's religions must not be subjected to the pressures of government for change each time a new political administration is elected to office. Under that Amendment's prohibition against governmental establishment of religion, as reinforced by the provisions of the Fourteenth Amendment, government in this country, be it state or federal, is without power to prescribe by law any particular form of prayer which is to be used as an official prayer in carrying on any program of governmentally sponsored religious activity.

There can be no doubt that New York's state prayer program officially establishes the religious beliefs embodied in the Regents' prayer. The [Board's] argument to the contrary, which is largely based upon the contention that the Regents' prayer is "non-denominational" and the fact that the program, as modified and approved by state courts, does not require all pupils to recite the prayer but permits those who wish to do so to remain silent or be excused from the room, ignores the essential nature of the program's constitutional defects. Neither the fact that the prayer may be denominationally neutral nor the fact that its observance on the part of the students is voluntary can serve to free it from the limitations of the Establishment Clause, as it might from the Free Exercise Clause, of the First Amendment, both of which are operative against the States by virtue of the Fourteenth Amendment. Although these two clauses may in certain instances overlap, they forbid two quite different kinds of governmental encroachment upon religious freedom. The Establishment Clause, unlike the Free Exercise Clause, does not depend upon any showing of direct governmental compulsion and is violated by the enactment of laws which establish an official religion whether those laws operate directly to coerce nonobserving individuals or not. This is not to say, of course, that laws officially prescribing a particular form of religious worship do not involve coercion of such individuals. When the power, prestige and financial support of government is placed behind a particular religious belief, the indirect coercive pressure upon religious minorities to conform to the prevailing officially approved religion is plain. But the purposes underlying the Establishment Clause go much further than that. Its first and most immediate purpose rested on the belief that a union of government and religion tends to destroy government and to degrade religion. The history of governmentally established religion, both in England and in this country, showed that whenever government had allied itself with one particular form of religion, the inevitable result had been that it had incurred the hatred, disrespect and even contempt of those who held contrary beliefs. That same history showed that many people had lost their respect for any religion that had relied upon the support of government to spread its faith. The Establishment Clause thus stands as an expression of principle on the part of the Founders of our Constitution that religion is too personal, too sacred, too holy, to permit its "unhallowed perversion" by a civil magistrate. Another purpose of the Establishment Clause rested upon an awareness of the historical fact that governmentally established religions and religious persecutions go hand in hand. The Founders knew that only a few years after the Book of Common Prayer became the only accepted form of religious services in the established Church of England, an Act of Uniformity was passed to compel all Englishmen to attend those services and to make it a criminal offense to conduct or attend religious gatherings of any other kind - a law which was

consistently flouted by dissenting religious groups in England and which contributed to widespread persecutions of
people like John Bunyan who persisted in holding
"unlawful [religious] meetings . . . to the great disturbance
and distraction of the good subjects of this kingdom. . . ."
And they knew that similar persecutions had received the
sanction of law in several of the colonies in this country
soon after the establishment of official religions in those
colonies. It was in large part to get completely away from
this sort of systematic religious persecution that the
Founders brought into being our Nation, our Constitution,
and our Bill of Rights with its prohibition against any
governmental establishment of religion. The New York
laws officially prescribing the Regents' prayer are inconsistent both with the purposes of the Establishment Clause
and with the Establishment Clause itself.

It has been argued that to apply the Constitution in such a
way as to prohibit state laws respecting an establishment
of religious services in public schools is to indicate a hos-
tility toward religion or toward prayer. Nothing, of
course, could be more wrong. The history of man is in-
separable from the history of religion. And perhaps it is
not too much to say that since the beginning of that history many people have devoutly believed that "More things
are wrought by prayer than this world dreams of." It was
doubtless largely due to men who believed this that there
grew up a sentiment that caused men to leave the cross-
currents of officially established state religions and religious persecution in Europe and come to this country
filled with the hope that they could find a place in which
they could pray when they pleased to the God of their
faith in the language they chose. And there were men of
this same faith in the power of prayer who led the fight
for adoption of our Constitution and also for our Bill of

Rights with the very guarantees of religious freedom that forbid the sort of governmental activity which New York has attempted here. These men knew that the First Amendment, which tried to put an end to governmental control of religion and of prayer, was not written to destroy either. They knew rather that it was written to quiet well-justified fears which nearly all of them felt arising out of an awareness that governments of the past had shackled men's tongues to make them speak only the religious thoughts that government wanted them to speak and to pray only to the God that government wanted them to pray to. It is neither sacrilegious nor antireligious to say that each separate government in this country should stay out of the business of writing or sanctioning official prayers and leave that purely religious function to the people themselves and to those the people choose to look to for religious guidance.

It is true that New York's establishment of its Regents' prayer as an officially approved religious doctrine of that State does not amount to a total establishment of one particular religious sect to the exclusion of all others - that, indeed, the governmental endorsement of that prayer seems relatively insignificant when compared to the governmental encroachments upon religion which were commonplace 200 years ago. To those who may subscribe to the view that because the Regents' official prayer is so brief and general there can be no danger to religious freedom in its governmental establishment, however, it may be appropriate to say in the words of James Madison, the author of the First Amendment:

> "[I]t is proper to take alarm at the first experiment on our liberties. . . . Who does not see that the same authority which can estab-

lish Christianity, in exclusion of all other Religions, may establish with the same ease any particular sect of Christians, in exclusion of all other Sects? That the same authority which can force a citizen to contribute three pence only of his property for the support of any one establishment, may force him to conform to any other establishment in all cases whatsoever?"

The judgment of the Court of Appeals of New York is reversed and the cause remanded [sent back to the appropriate lower court for reruling].

JUSTICE POTTER STEWART, dissenting: A local school board in New York has provided that those pupils who wish to do so may join in a brief prayer at the beginning of each school day, acknowledging their dependence upon God and asking His blessing upon them and upon their parents, their teachers, and their country. The Court today decides that in permitting this brief nondenominational prayer the school board has violated the Constitution of the United States. I think this decision is wrong.

The Court does not hold, nor could it, that New York has interfered with the free exercise of anybody's religion. For the state courts have made clear that those who object to reciting the prayer must be entirely free of any compulsion to do so, including any "embarrassments and pressures." But the Court says that in permitting school children to say this simple prayer, the New York authorities have established "an official religion."

With all respect, I think the Court has misapplied a great constitutional principle. I cannot see how an "official religion" is established by letting those who want to say a prayer say it. On the contrary, I think that to deny the wish of these school children to join in reciting this prayer is to deny them the opportunity of sharing in the spiritual heritage of our Nation.

The Court's historical review of the quarrels over the Book of Common Prayer in England throws no light for me on the issue before us in this case. England had then and has now an established church. Equally unenlightening, I think, is the history of the early establishment and later rejection of an official church in our own States. For we deal here not with the establishment of a state church, which would, of course, be constitutionally impermissible, but with whether school children who want to begin their day by joining in prayer must be prohibited from doing so. Moreover, I think that the Court's task, in this as in all areas of constitutional adjudication, is not responsibly aided by the uncritical invocation of metaphors like the "wall of separation," a phrase nowhere to be found in the Constitution. What is relevant to the issue here is not the history of an established church in sixteenth century England or in eighteenth century America, but the history of the religious traditions of our people, reflected in countless practices of the institutions and officials of our government.

At the opening of each day's Session of this Court we stand, while one of our officials invokes the protection of God. Since the days of John Marshall our Crier has said, "God save the United States and this Honorable Court." Both the Senate and the House of Representatives open their daily Sessions with prayer. Each of our Presidents, from George Washington to John F. Kennedy, has upon assuming his Office asked the protection and help of God.

The Court today says that the state and federal governments are without constitutional power to prescribe any
particular form of words to be recited by any group of
the American people on any subject touching religion.
One of the stanzas of "The Star-Spangled Banner," made
our National Anthem by Act of Congress in 1931, contains these verses:

> "Blest with victory and peace, may the
>   heav'n rescued land
> Praise the Pow'r that hath made and pre-
>   served us a nation!
> Then conquer we must, when our cause it is
>   just,
> And this be our motto 'In God is our
>   Trust.'"

In 1954 Congress added a phrase to the Pledge of Alle-
giance to the Flag so that it now contains the words "one
Nation *under God*, indivisible, with liberty and justice for
all."   In 1952 Congress enacted legislation calling upon
the President each year to proclaim a National Day of
Prayer.   Since 1865 the words "IN GOD WE TRUST"
have been impressed on our coins.

Countless similar examples could be listed, but there is no
need to belabor the obvious. It was all summed up by this
Court just ten years ago in a single sentence: "We are a
religious people whose institutions presuppose a Supreme
Being."

I do not believe that this Court, or the Congress, or the
President has by the actions and practices I have men-
tioned established an "official religion" in violation of the
Constitution. And I do not believe the State of New York

has done so in this case. What each has done has been to recognize and to follow the deeply entrenched and highly cherished spiritual traditions of our Nation - traditions which come down to us from those who almost two hundred years ago avowed [in the Declaration of Independence] their "firm Reliance on the Protection of divine Providence" when they proclaimed the freedom and independence of this brave new world.

I dissent.

FAIR TRIALS

GIDEON v. WAINWRIGHT

The Fair Trials Decision case originates in Florida. In June 1961, Clarence Gideon was arrested and charged with breaking and entering in Bay Harbor. He was tried in a Florida Circuit Court in August 1961. Gideon stated in Court that he was unable to afford a lawyer and asked the Judge to appoint one for him. The Judge denied his request. In Florida, at that time, only poor defendants in capital cases [where the death penalty might be imposed] were entitled to Court-appointed legal representation. Without legal counsel, Gideon put on his own defense, was convicted, and was sentenced to prison.

Gideon appealed for his release to the Florida Supreme Court on the ground that his conviction violated his rights under the Federal Constitution. The Florida Supreme Court refused and Gideon appealed in a penciled, longhand letter to the U.S. Supreme Court, which agreed to review his conviction.

Oral arguments were heard on January 15, 1962 and a decision was announced on March 18, 1963.

Justice Hugo Black delivered the opinion of the Court. Justices William Douglas, John Marshall Harlan and William Clark concurred.

The full text of *Gideon v. Wainwright* can be found in United States Reports, volume 372, page 335.

GIDEON v. WAINWRIGHT

March 18, 1963

JUSTICE HUGO BLACK: Petitioner [Clarence Gideon] was charged in a Florida state court with having broken and entered a poolroom with intent to commit a misdemeanor. This offense is a felony under Florida law. Appearing in court without funds and without a lawyer, petitioner asked the court to appoint counsel for him, whereupon the following colloquy took place:

> "The Court: Mr. Gideon, I am sorry, but I cannot appoint Counsel to represent you in this case. Under the laws of the State of Florida, the only time the Court can appoint Counsel to represent a Defendant is when that person is charged with a capital offense [one carrying a possible death penalty]. I am sorry, but I will have to deny your request to appoint Counsel to defend you in this case.

> "The Defendant: The United States Supreme Court says I am entitled to be represented by Counsel."

Put to trial before a jury, Gideon conducted his defense about as well as could be expected from a layman. He made an opening statement to the jury, cross-examined the State's witnesses, presented witnesses in his own defense, declined to testify himself, and made a short argument "emphasizing his innocence to the charge contained in the Information filed in this case." The jury returned a verdict of guilty, and petitioner was sentenced to serve

five years in the state prison. Later, petitioner filed in the
Florida Supreme Court this habeas corpus [questioning
the legality of his imprisonment] petition [against Wainwright, the Director of Corrections] attacking his conviction and sentence on the ground that the trial court's refusal to appoint counsel for him denied him rights
"guaranteed by the Constitution and the Bill of Rights by
the United States Government." . . . [T]he State Supreme
Court [refused his petition]. Since 1942, when *Betts v.
Brady* was decided by a divided Court, the problem of a
defendant's federal constitutional right to counsel in a
state court has been a continuing source of controversy
and litigation in both state and federal courts. To give
this problem anther review here, we granted certiorari [a
review]. Since Gideon was proceeding in forma pauperis
[without funds], we appointed counsel to represent him
and requested both sides to discuss in their briefs and oral
arguments the following: "Should this Court's holding in
Betts v. Brady be reconsidered?"

The facts upon which Betts claimed that he had been unconstitutionally denied the right to have counsel appointed to assist him are strikingly like the facts upon which
Gideon here bases his federal constitutional claim. Betts
was indicted for robbery in a Maryland state court. On
arraignment, he told the trial judge of his lack of funds to
hire a lawyer and asked the court to appoint one for him.
Betts was advised that it was not the practice in that county to appoint counsel for indigent defendants except in
murder and rape cases. He then pleaded not guilty, had
witnesses summoned, cross-examined the State's witnesses,
examined his own, and chose not to testify himself. He
was found guilty by the judge, sitting without a jury, and
sentenced to eight years in prison. Like Gideon, Betts
sought release by habeas corpus, alleging that he had been

denied the right to assistance of counsel in violation of
the Fourteenth Amendment. Betts was denied any relief,
and on review this Court affirmed [let the lower court
ruling stand]. It was held that a refusal to appoint counsel
for an indigent defendant charged with a felony did not
necessarily violate the Due Process Clause of the Fourteenth Amendment, which for reasons given the Court
deemed to be the only applicable federal constitutional
provision. The Court said:

> "Asserted denial [of due process] is to be
> tested by an appraisal of the totality of
> facts in a given case. That which may, in
> one setting, constitute a denial of funda-
> mental fairness, shocking to the universal
> sense of justice, may, in other circum-
> stances, and in the light of other considera-
> tions, fall short of such denial."

Treating due process as "a concept less rigid and more
fluid than those envisaged in other specific and particular
provisions of the Bill of Rights," the Court held that refusal to appoint counsel under the particular facts and circumstances in the *Betts* case was not so "offensive to the
common and fundamental ideas of fairness" as to amount
to a denial of due process. Since the facts and circumstances of the two cases are so nearly indistinguishable, we
think the *Betts v. Brady* holding if left standing would require us to reject Gideon's claim that the Constitution
guarantees him the assistance of counsel. Upon full reconsideration we conclude that *Betts v. Brady* should be
overruled.

The Sixth Amendment provides, "In all criminal prosecutions, the accused shall enjoy the right . . . to have the As-

sistance of Counsel for his defence." We have construed
this to mean that in federal courts counsel must be provided for defendants unable to employ counsel unless the
right is competently and intelligently waived. Betts argued that this right is extended to indigent defendants in
state courts by the Fourteenth Amendment. In response
the Court stated that, while the Sixth Amendment laid
down "no rule for the conduct of the States, the question
recurs whether the constraint laid by the Amendment
upon the national courts expresses a rule so fundamental
and essential to a fair trial, and so, to due process of law,
that it is made obligatory upon the States by the Fourteenth Amendment." In order to decide whether the Sixth
Amendment's guarantee of counsel is of this fundamental
nature, the Court in *Betts* set out and considered
"[r]elevant data on the subject . . . afforded by constitutional and statutory provisions subsisting in the colonies
and the States prior to the inclusion of the Bill of Rights
in the national Constitution, and in the constitutional, legislative, and judicial history of the States to the present
date." On the basis of this historical data the Court concluded that "appointment of counsel is not a fundamental
right, essential to a fair trial." It was for this reason the
Betts Court refused to accept the contention that the Sixth
Amendment's guarantee of counsel for indigent federal
defendants was extended to or, in the words of that Court,
"made obligatory upon the States by the Fourteenth
Amendment." Plainly, had the Court concluded that appointment of counsel for an indigent criminal defendant
was "a fundamental right, essential to a fair trial," it
would have held that the Fourteenth Amendment requires
appointment of counsel in a state court, just as the Sixth
Amendment requires in a federal court. We think the
Court in *Betts* had ample precedent for acknowledging
that those guarantees of the Bill of Rights which are fun-

damental safeguards of liberty immune from federal
abridgment are equally protected against state invasion by
the Due Process Clause of the Fourteenth Amendment. . . .
[In] *Powell v. Alabama* (1932) . . . the Court held that . . .
the Fourteenth Amendment [to the Constitution]
"embraced" those "fundamental principles of liberty and
justice which lie at the base of all our civil and political
institutions,'" even though they had been "specifically
dealt with in another part of the federal Constitution." In
many cases other than *Powell* and *Betts*, this Court has
looked to the fundamental nature of original Bill of
Rights guarantees to decide whether the Fourteenth
Amendment makes them obligatory on the States. Explicitly recognized to be of this "fundamental nature" and
therefore made immune from state invasion by the Fourteenth, or some part of it, are the First Amendment's freedoms of speech, press, religion, assembly, association, and
petition for redress of grievances. For the same reason . .
. the Court has made obligatory on the States the Fifth
Amendment's command that private property shall not be
taken for public use without just compensation, the
Fourth Amendment's prohibition of unreasonable searches and seizures, and the Eight's ban on cruel and unusual
punishment. On the other hand, this Court in *Palko v.
Connecticut* refused to hold that the Fourteenth Amendment made the double jeopardy provision of the Fifth
Amendment obligatory on the States. In so refusing, however, the Court, speaking through Justice Cardozo, was
careful to emphasize that "immunities that are valid as
against the federal government by force of the specific
pledges of particular amendments have been found to be
implicit in the concept of ordered liberty, and thus,
through the Fourteenth Amendment, become valid as
against the states." . . .

We accept *Betts v. Brady*'s assumption, based as it was on
our prior cases, that a provision of the Bill of Rights
which is "fundamental and essential to a fair trial" is made
obligatory upon the States by the Fourteenth Amendment.
We think the Court in *Betts* was wrong, however, in concluding that the Sixth Amendment's guarantee of counsel
is not one of these fundamental rights. Ten years before
Betts v. Brady, this court . . . had unequivocally declared
that "the right to the aid of counsel is of this fundamental
character."   While the Court [limited] its holding to the
particular facts and circumstances of that case, its conclusions about the fundamental nature of the right to counsel
are unmistakable. Several years later, in 1936 [in *Gros-
jean v. American Press*], the Court reemphasized what it
had said about the fundamental nature of the right to
counsel in this language:

> "We concluded that certain fundamental
> rights, safeguarded by the first eight
> amendments against federal action, were
> also safeguarded against state action by the
> due process of law clause of the Fourteenth
> Amendment, and among them the funda-
> mental right of the accused to the aid of
> counsel in a criminal prosecution."

And again in 1938 [in *Johnson v. Zerbst*] this Court said:

> "[The assistance of counsel] is one of the
> safeguards of the Sixth Amendment deemed
> necessary to insure fundamental human
> rights of life and liberty. . . . The Sixth
> Amendment stands as a constant admonition
> that if the constitutional safeguards it pro-
> vides be lost, justice will not 'still be done.'"

In light of these and many other prior decisions of this Court, it is not surprising that the *Betts* Court, when faced with the contention that "one charged with crime, who is unable to obtain counsel, must be furnished counsel by the State," conceded that "[e]xpressions in the opinions of this court lend color to the argument. . . ." The fact is that in deciding as it did - that "appointment of counsel is not a fundamental right, essential to a fair trial" - the Court in *Betts v. Brady* made an abrupt break with its own well-considered precedents. In returning to these old precedents, sounder we believe than the new, we but restore constitutional principles established to achieve a fair system of justice. Not only these precedents but also reason and reflection require us to recognize that in our adversary system of criminal justice, any person haled into court, who is too poor to hire a lawyer, cannot be assured a fair trial unless counsel is provided for him. This seems to us to be an obvious truth. Governments, both state and federal, quite properly spend vast sums of money to establish machinery to try defendants accused of crime. Lawyers to prosecute are everywhere deemed essential to protect the public's interest in an orderly society. Similarly, there are few defendants charged with crime, few indeed, who fail to hire the best lawyers they can get to prepare and present their defenses. That government hires lawyers to prosecute and defendants who have the money hire lawyers to defend are the strongest indications of the widespread belief that lawyers in criminal courts are necessities, not luxuries. The right of one charged with crime to counsel may not be deemed fundamental and essential to fair trials in some countries, but it is in ours. From the very beginning, our state and national constitutions and laws have laid great emphasis on procedural and substantive safeguards designed to assure fair trials before impartial tribunals in which every defendant stands equal before the law. This noble ideal cannot be realized if the poor man charged with crime has to face his accusers without a lawyer to assist him. A defendant's need for a lawyer is nowhere better stated than in the moving words of Justice Sutherland in *Powell v. Alabama*: "The right to be heard would be, in many cases, of little avail if it did not comprehend the right to be heard by counsel. Even the intelligent and educated layman has small and sometimes no skill in the science of law. If charged with crime, he is incapable, generally, of determining for himself whether the indictment is good or bad. He is unfamiliar with the rules of evidence. Left without the aid of counsel he may be put on trial without a proper charge, and convicted upon incompetent evidence, or evidence irrelevant to the issue or otherwise inadmissible. He lacks both the skill and knowledge adequately to prepare his defense, even though he have a perfect one. He requires the guiding hand of counsel at every step in the proceedings against him. Without it, though he be not guilty, he faces the danger of conviction because he does not know how to establish his innocence."

The Court in *Betts v. Brady* departed from the sound wisdom upon which the Court's holding in *Powell v. Alabama* rested. Florida, supported by two other States, has asked that *Betts v. Brady* be left intact. Twenty-two States, as friends of the Court, argue that *Betts* was "an anachronism when handed down" and that it should now be overruled. We agree.

Reversed.

SEXUAL PRIVACY

GRISWOLD v. CONNECTICUT

The Sexual Privacy Decision originates in Connecticut. In November 1961, Griswold was the Director of the Planned Parenthood League of Connecticut. Dr. Buxton, a licensed physician and a professor of medicine at Yale University, served as the Medical Director for the League at their Center in New Haven.

Both were arrested, tried, found guilty and fined for violating a Connecticut law prohibiting the giving of information, instruction, or medical advice on contraception to married persons.

They appealed their convictions to the Appellate Division of the Connecticut Circuit Court and to the Connecticut Supreme Court of Errors, losing in both courts. They then appealed to the U.S. Supreme Court which agreed to a review.

Oral arguments were heard March 29 -30, 1965 and a decision was announced June 7, 1965.

Justice William Douglas delivered the opinion of the Court. Justice Arthur Goldberg wrote a concurring opinion which was joined into by Chief Justice Earl Warren and Justice William Brennan. Justices John Marshall Harlan and Byron White Concurred. Justices Hugo Black and Potter Stewart dissented.

The complete text of *Griswold v. Connecticut* can be found in United States Reports, volume 381, page 479.

GRISWOLD v. CONNECTICUT

June 7, 1965

JUSTICE WILLIAM DOUGLAS: Appellant Griswold is Executive Director of the Planned Parenthood League of Connecticut. Appellant Buxton is a licensed physician and a professor at the Yale Medical School who served as Medical Director for the League at its Center in New Haven - a center open and operating from November 1 to November 10, 1961, when appellants were arrested.

They gave information, instruction, and medical advice to *married persons* as to the means of preventing conception. They examined the wife and prescribed the best contraceptive device or material for her use. Fees were usually charged, although some couples were serviced free.

The statutes whose constitutionality is involved in this appeal are [Sections] 53-32 and 54-196 of the General Statutes of Connecticut (1958 revision). The former provides: "Any person who uses any drug, medicinal article or instrument for the purpose of preventing conception shall be fined not less than fifty dollars or imprisoned not less than sixty days nor more than one year or be both fined and imprisoned."

Section 54-196 provides: "Any person who assists, abets, counsels, causes, hires or commands another to commit any offense may be prosecuted and punished as if he were the principal offender."

The appellants were found guilty as accessories [persons who aid in a crime] and fined $100 each, against [their] claim that the accessory statute as so applied violated the Fourteenth Amendment.

We think that appellants have standing [the right] to raise the constitutional rights of the married people with whom they had a professional relationship. . . .

The rights of husband and wife, pressed here, are likely to be diluted or adversely affected unless those rights are considered in a suit involving those who have this kind of confidential relation to them.

Coming to the merits, we are met with a wide range of questions that implicate the Due Process Clause of the Fourteenth Amendment. . . . We do not sit as a super-legislature to determine the wisdom, need, and propriety of laws that touch economic problems, business affairs, or social conditions. This law, however, operates directly on an intimate relation of husband and wife and their physician's role in one aspect of that relation.

The association of people is not mentioned in the Constitution nor in the Bill of Rights. The right to educate a child in a school of the parents' choice - whether public or private or parochial - is also not mentioned. Nor is the right to study any particular subject or any foreign language. Yet the First Amendment has been construed to include certain of those rights.

. . . . [T]he State may not, consistently with the spirit of the First Amendment, contract the spectrum of available knowledge. The right of freedom of speech and press includes not only the right to utter or to print, but the right to distribute, the right to receive, the right to read and freedom of inquiry, freedom of thought, and freedom to teach - indeed the freedom of the entire university community.   Without those peripheral rights the specific rights would be less secure. . . .

In *NAACP v. Alabama*, we protected the "freedom to associate and privacy in one's associations," noting that freedom of association was a peripheral First Amendment right. Disclosure of membership lists of a constitutionally valid association, we held, was invalid "as entailing the likelihood of a substantial restraint upon the exercise by petitioner's members of their right to freedom of association." In other words, the First Amendment has a penumbra where privacy is protected from governmental intrusion.   In like context, we have protected forms of "association" that are not political in the customary sense but pertain to the social, legal, and economic benefit of the members. In *Schware v. Board of Bar Examiners*, we held it not permissible to bar a lawyer from practice, because he had once been a member of the Communist Party. The man's "association with that Party" was not shown to be "anything more than a political faith in a political party" and was not action of a kind proving bad moral character.

Those cases involved more than the "right of assembly" - a right that extends to all irrespective of their race or ideology. The right of "association," like the right of belief, is more than the right to attend a meeting; it includes the right to express one's attitudes or philosophies by membership in a group or by affiliation with it or by other lawful means. Association in that context is a form of expression of opinion; and while it is not expressly included in the First Amendment its existence is necessary in making the express guarantees fully meaningful.

The foregoing cases suggest that specific guarantees in the Bill of Rights have penumbras, formed by emanations from those guarantees that help give them life and substance. Various guarantees create zones of privacy. The right of association contained in the penumbra of the First Amendment is one, as we have seen. The Third Amendment in its prohibition against the quartering of soldiers "in any house" in time of peace without the consent of the owner is another facet of that privacy. The Fourth Amendment explicitly affirms the "right of the people to be secure in their persons, houses, papers, and effects, against unreasonable searches and seizures." The Fifth Amendment in its Self-Incrimination Clause enables the citizen to create a zone of privacy which government may not force him to surrender to his detriment. The Ninth Amendment provides: "The enumeration in the Constitution, of certain rights, shall not be construed to deny or disparage others retained by the people."

The Fourth and Fifth Amendments were described in *Boyd v. United States* as protection against all governmental invasions "of the sanctity of a man's home and the privacies of life." We recently referred in *Mapp v. Ohio* to the Fourth Amendment as creating a "right to privacy, no less important than any other right carefully and particularly reserved to the people."

We have had many controversies over these penumbral rights of "privacy and repose." These cases bear witness that the right of privacy which presses for recognition here is a legitimate one.

The present case, then, concerns a relationship laying within the zone of privacy created by several fundamental constitutional guarantees. And it concerns a law which, in forbidding the *use* of contraceptives rather than regulating their manufacture or sale, seeks to achieve its goals by means having a maximum destructive impact upon that relationship. Such a law cannot stand in light of the familiar principle, so often applied by this Court, that a "governmental purpose to control or prevent activities constitutionally subject to state regulation may not be achieved by means which sweep unnecessarily broadly and thereby invade the area of protected freedoms." Would we allow the police to search the sacred precincts of marital bedrooms for telltale signs of the use of contraceptives? The very idea is repulsive to the notions of privacy surrounding the marriage relationship.

We deal with a right of privacy older than the Bill of Rights - older than our political parties, older than our school system. Marriage is a coming together for better or for worse, hopefully enduring, and intimate to the degree of being sacred. It is an association that promotes a way of life, not causes; a harmony in living, not political faiths; a bilateral loyalty, not commercial or social projects. Yet it is an association for as noble a purpose as any involved in our prior decisions. *Reversed.*

CENSORSHIP

NEW YORK TIMES v. UNITED STATES

The Censorship Decision originates during the Nixon Presidency. The New York Times and Washington Post obtained a copies of a classified study entitled, "History of U.S. Decision-Making Process on Viet Nam Policy", which eventually came to be know as The Pentagon Papers.

The United States Government, upon learning that the Times and Post intended to publish the Pentagon Papers attempted to obtain injunctions [orders halting publication] from U.S. District Courts in New York and Washington, D.C.

The New York District Court refused and the Government appealed to the U.S. Court of Appeals in New York which issued the injunction against The Times. The Washington District Court refused to issue an injunction against the Post as did the U.S. Court of Appeals in Washington. The Times appealed the ruling of the New York Court and the Government appealed the ruling of the Washington Court. The the Supreme Court granted a review to both.

Oral arguments were heard June 26 and a decision was announced June 30, 1971.

The decision of the Court was announced Per Curiam [by the Court]. Concurring opinions were issued by Justices Hugo Black, William Douglas, William Brennan, Potter Stewart, Byron White, and Thurgood Marshall. Dissenting opinions were issued by Chief Justice Warren Burger and Justices John Harlan and Harry Blackmun.

The complete text of *New York Times v. United States* can be found in United States Reports, volume 403, page 713.

NEW YORK TIMES v. UNITED STATES

June 30, 1971

PER CURIAM [by the Court]: We granted certiorari [agreed to review] these cases in which the United States seeks to enjoin [stop] the New York Times and the Washington Post from publishing the contents of a classified study entitled "History of U.S. Decision-Making Process on Viet Nam Policy" [The Pentagon Papers].

"Any system of prior restraints of expression [stopping of publication] comes to this Court bearing a heavy presumption against its constitutional validity." The Government "thus carries a heavy burden of showing justification for the imposition of such a restraint." The District Court for the Southern District of New York in the *New York Times* case and the District Court . . . and the Court of Appeals for the District of Columbia Circuit in the *Washington Post* case held that the Government had not met that burden. We agree.

The judgment of the Court of Appeals for the District of Columbia Circuit is therefore affirmed [let stand]. The order of the Court of Appeals for the Second circuit is reversed and the case is remanded [returned to the lower court for reruling].

JUSTICE HUGO BLACK, joined by JUSTICE WILLIAM DOUGLAS, concurring: I adhere to the view that the Government's case against the Washington Post should have been dismissed and that the injunction against the New York Times should have been vacated [cancelled] without oral argument when the cases were first presented to this Court. I believe that every moment's continu-

ance of the injunctions against these newspapers amounts
to a flagrant, indefensible, and continuing violation of the
First Amendment. . . . In my view it is unfortunate that
some of my Brethren are apparently willing to hold that
the publication of news may sometimes be enjoined. Such
a holding would make a shambles of the First Amendment.

Our Government was launched in 1789 with the adoption
of the Constitution. The Bill of Rights, including the
First Amendment, followed in 1791. Now, for the first
time in the 182 years since the founding of the Republic,
the federal courts are asked to hold that the First Amendment does not mean what it says, but rather means that
the Government can halt the publication of current news
of vital importance to the people of this country.

In seeking injunctions against these newspapers and in its
presentation to the Court, the Executive Branch seems to
have forgotten the essential purpose and history of the
First Amendment. When the Constitution was adopted,
many people strongly opposed it because the document
contained no Bill of Rights to safeguard certain basic
freedoms. They especially feared that the new powers
granted to a central government might be interpreted to
permit the government to curtail freedom of religion,
press, assembly, and speech. In response to an overwhelm-
ing public clamor, James Madison offered a series of
amendments to satisfy citizens that these great liberties
would remain safe and beyond the power of government
to abridge. Madison proposed what later became the First
Amendment in three parts, two of which are set out below, and one of which proclaimed: "The people shall not
be deprived or abridged of their right to speak, to write,
or to publish their sentiments; *and the freedom of the*

press, as one of the great bulwarks of liberty, shall be inviolable." The amendments were offered to *curtail* and *restrict* the general powers granted to the Executive, Legislative, and Judicial Branches two years before in the original Constitution. The Bill of Rights changed the original Constitution into a new charter under which no branch of government could abridge the people's freedoms of press, speech, religion, and assembly. Yet the Solicitor General [the Government's lawyer] argues and some members of the Court appear to agree that the general powers of the Government adopted in the original Constitution should be interpreted to limit and restrict the specific and emphatic guarantees of the Bill of Rights adopted later. I can imagine no greater perversion of history. Madison and the other Framers of the First Amendment, able men that they were, wrote in language they earnestly believed could never be misunderstood: "Congress shall make no law . . . abridging the freedom . . of the press. . . ." Both the history and language of the First Amendment support the view that the press must be left free to publish news, whatever the source, without censorship, injunctions, or prior restraints.

In the First Amendment the Founding Fathers gave the free press the protection it must have to fulfill its essential role in our democracy. The press was to serve the governed, not the governors. The Government's power to censor the press was abolished so that the press would remain forever free to censure the Government. The press was protected so that it could bare the secrets of government and inform the people. Only a free and unrestrained press can effectively expose deception in government. And paramount among the responsibilities of a free press is the duty to prevent any part of the government from deceiving the people and sending them off to distant lands to die of foreign fevers and foreign shot and shell. In my view, far from deserving condemnation for their courageous reporting, the New York Times, the Washington Post, and other newspapers should be commended for serving the purpose that the Founding Fathers saw so clearly. In revealing the workings of government that led to the Vietnam war, the newspapers nobly did precisely that which the Founders hoped and trusted they would do.

The Government's case here is based on premises entirely different from those that guided the Framers of the First Amendment. The Solicitor General has carefully and emphatically stated:

> "Now, Mr. Justice [Black], your construction of . . . [the First Amendment] is well known, and I certainly respect it. You say that no law means no law, and that should be obvious. I can only say, Mr. Justice, that to me it is equally obvious that 'no law' does not mean 'no law', and I would seek to persuade the Court that that is true. . . . [T]here are other parts of the Constitution that grant powers and responsibilities to the Executive, and . . . the First Amendment was not intended to make it impossible for the Executive to function or to protect the security of the United States."

And the Government argues . . . that in spite of the First Amendment, "[t]he authority of the Executive Department to protect the nation against publication of information whose disclosure would endanger the national security stems from two interrelated sources: the constitutional power of the President over the conduct of foreign affairs and his authority as Commander-in-Chief."

In other words, we are asked to hold that despite the First Amendment's emphatic command, the Executive Branch, the Congress, and the Judiciary can make laws enjoining publication of current news and abridging freedom of the press in the name of "national security." The Government does not even attempt to rely on any act of Congress. Instead it makes the bold and dangerously far-reaching contention that the courts should take it upon themselves to "make" a law abridging freedom of the press in the name of equity, presidential power and national security, even when the representatives of the people in Congress have adhered to the command of the First Amendment and refused to make such a law. To find that the President has "inherent power" to halt the publication of news by resort to the courts would wipe out the First Amendment and destroy the fundamental liberty and security of the very people the Government hopes to make "secure." No one can read the history of the adoption of the First Amendment without being convinced beyond any doubt that it was injunctions like those sought here that Madison and his collaborators intended to outlaw in this Nation for all time.

The word "security" is a broad, vague generality whose contours should not be invoked to abrogate the fundamental law embodied in the First Amendment. The guarding of military and diplomatic secrets at the expense of informed representative government provides no real security for our Republic. The Framers of the First Amendment, fully aware of both the need to defend a new nation and the abuses of the English and Colonial governments, sought to give this new society strength and security by providing that freedom of speech, press, religion, and assembly should not be abridged. This thought was eloquently expressed in 1937 by Chief Justice Hughes . . . when the Court held a man could not be punished for attending a meeting run by Communists.

> "The greater the importance of safeguarding the community from incitements to the overthrow of our institutions by force and violence, the more imperative is the need to preserve inviolate the constitutional rights of free speech, free press and free assembly in order to maintain the opportunity for free political discussion, to the end that government may be responsive to the will of the people and that changes, if desired, may be obtained by peaceful means. Therein lies the security of the Republic, the very foundation of constitutional government."

JUSTICE POTTER STEWART, concurring: In the governmental structure created by our Constitution, the Executive is endowed with enormous power in the two related areas of national defense and international relations. This power, largely unchecked by the Legislative and Judicial branches, has been pressed to the very hilt since the advent of the nuclear missile age. For better or for worse, the simple fact is that a President of the United States possesses vastly greater constitutional independence in these two vital areas of power than does, say, a prime minister of a country with a parliamentary form of government.

In the absence of the governmental checks and balances present in other areas of our national life, the only effec-

tive restraint upon executive policy and power in the
areas of national defense and international affairs may lie
in an enlightened citizenry - in an informed and critical
public opinion which alone can here protect the values of
democratic government. For this reason, it is perhaps
here that a press that is alert, aware, and free most vitally
serves the basic purpose of the First Amendment. For
without an informed and free press there cannot be an enlightened people.

Yet it is elementary that the successful conduct of international diplomacy and the maintenance of an effective
national defense require both confidentiality and secrecy.
Other nations can hardly deal with this Nation in an atmosphere of mutual trust unless they can be assured that
their confidences will be kept. And within our own executive departments, the development of considered and intelligent international policies would be impossible if
those charged with their formulation could not communicate with each other freely, frankly, and in confidence. In
the area of basic national defense the frequent need for
absolute secrecy is, of course, self-evident.

I think there can be but one answer to this dilemma, if dilemma it be. The responsibility must be where the power
is. If the Constitution gives the Executive a large degree
of unshared power in the conduct of foreign affairs and
the maintenance of our national defense, then under the
Constitution the Executive must have the largely unshared duty to determine and preserve the degree of internal security necessary to exercise that power successfully.
It is an awesome responsibility, requiring judgment and
wisdom of a high order. I should suppose that moral, political, and practical considerations would dictate that a
very first principle of that wisdom would be an insistence

upon avoiding secrecy for its own sake. For when everything is classified, then nothing is classified, and the system becomes one to be disregarded by the cynical or the
careless, and to be manipulated by those intent on self-
protection or self-promotion. I should suppose, in short,
that the hallmark of a truly effective internal security
system would be the maximum possible disclosure, recognizing that secrecy can best be preserved only when credi-
bility is truly maintained. But be that as it may, it is clear
to me that it is the constitutional duty of the Executive -
as a matter of sovereign prerogative and not as a matter
of law as the courts know law - through the promulgation
and enforcement of executive regulations, to protect the
confidentiality necessary to carry out its responsibilities in
the fields of international relations and national defense.

This is not to say that Congress and the courts have no
role to play. Undoubtedly Congress has the power to enact specific and appropriate criminal laws to protect government property and preserve government secrets. Congress has passed such laws, and several of them are of
very colorable relevance to the apparent circumstances of
these cases. And if a criminal prosecution is instituted, it
will be the responsibility of the courts to decide the applicability of the criminal law under which the charge is
brought. . . .

. . . . We are asked . . . to perform a function that the
Constitution gave to the Executive, not the Judiciary. We
are asked, quite simply, to prevent the publication by two
newspapers of material that the Executive Branch insists
should not, in the national interest, be published. I am
convinced that the Executive is correct with respect to
some of the documents involved. But I cannot say that
disclosure of any of them will surely result in direct, im-

mediate, and irreparable damage to our Nation or its people. That being so, there can under the First Amendment be but one judicial resolution of the issues before us.

JUSTICE THURGOOD MARSHALL, concurring: The Government contends that the only issue in these cases is whether in a suit by the United States, "the First Amendment bars a court from prohibiting a newspaper from publishing material whose disclosure would pose a 'grave and immediate danger to the security of the United States.'" With all due respect, I believe the ultimate issue in these cases is even more basic than the one posed by the Solicitor General. The issue is whether this Court or the Congress has the power to make law.

In these cases there is no problem concerning the President's power to classify information as "secret" or "top secret." Congress has specifically recognized Presidential authority . . . to classify documents and information. Nor is there any issue here regarding the President's power as Chief Executive and Commander in Chief to protect national security by disciplining employees who disclose information and by taking precautions to prevent leaks.

The problem here is whether in these particular cases the Executive Branch has authority to invoke the equity [justice administered according to fairness] jurisdiction of the courts to protect what it believes to be the national interest. The Government argues that in addition to the inherent power of any government to protect itself, the President's power to conduct foreign affairs and his position as Commander in Chief give him authority to impose censorship on the press to protect his ability to deal effectively with foreign nations and to conduct the military affairs of the country. Of course, it is beyond cavil that the

President has broad powers by virtue of his primary responsibility for the conduct of our foreign affairs and his
position as Commander in Chief. And in some situations
it may be that under whatever inherent powers the Government may have, as well as the implicit authority derived from the President's mandate to conduct foreign affairs and to act as Commander in Chief, there is a basis
for the invocation of the equity jurisdiction of this Court
as an aid to prevent the publication of material damaging
to "national security," however that term may be defined.

It would, however, be utterly inconsistent with the concept of separation of powers for this Court to use its power of contempt [punishing willful disregard of a court] to
prevent behavior that Congress has specifically declined
to prohibit. There would be a similar damage to the basic
concept of these co-equal branches of Government if
when the Executive Branch has adequate authority granted by Congress to protect "national security" it can choose
instead to invoke the contempt power of a court to enjoin
the threatened conduct. The constitution provides that
Congress shall make laws, the President execute laws, and
courts interpret laws. It did not provide for government
by injunction in which the courts and the Executive
Branch can "make law" without regard to the action of
Congress. It may be more convenient for the Executive
Branch if it need only convince a judge to prohibit conduct rather than ask the Congress to pass a law, and it
may be more convenient to enforce a contempt order than
to seek a criminal conviction in a jury trial. Moreover, it
may be considered politically wise to get a court to share
the responsibility for arresting those who the Executive
Branch has probable cause to believe are violating the law.
But convenience and political considerations of the mo-

ment do not justify a basic departure from the principles of our system of government.

In these cases we are not faced with a situation where Congress has failed to provide the Executive with broad power to protect the Nation from disclosure of damaging state secrets. Congress has on several occasions given extensive consideration to the problem of protecting the military and strategic secrets of the United States. This consideration has resulted in the enactment of statutes making it a crime to receive, disclose, communicate, withhold, and publish certain documents, photographs, instruments, appliances, and information. . . .

Even if it is determined that the Government could not in good faith bring criminal prosecutions against the New York Times and the Washington Post, it is clear that Congress has specifically rejected passing legislation that would have clearly given the President the power he seeks here and made the current activity of the newspapers unlawful. When Congress specifically declines to make conduct unlawful it is not for this Court to redecide those issues - to overrule Congress.

On at least two occasions Congress has refused to enact legislation that would have made the conduct engaged in here unlawful and given the President the power that he seeks in this case. In 1917 during the debate over the original Espionage Act, . . . Congress rejected a proposal to give the President in time of war or threat of war authority to directly prohibit by proclamation the publication of information relating to national defense that might be useful to the enemy. The proposal provided that:

"During any national emergency resulting
from a war to which the United States is a
party, or from threat of such a war, the
President may, by proclamation, declare the
existence of such emergency and, by proclamation, prohibit the publishing or commu-
nicating of, or the attempting to publish or
communicate any information relating to
the national defense which, in his judgment,
is of such character that it is or might be
useful to the enemy. Whoever violates any
such prohibition shall be punished by a fine
of not more than $10,000 or by imprison-
ment for not more than 10 years, or both:
Provided, That nothing in this section shall
be construed to limit or restrict any discussion, comment, or criticism of the acts or
policies of the Government or its representatives or the publication of the same."

Congress rejected this proposal after war against Germany
had been declared even though many believed that there
was a grave national emergency and that the threat of security leaks and espionage was serious. The Executive
Branch has not gone to Congress and requested that the
decision to provide such power be reconsidered. Instead,
the Executive Branch comes to this Court and asks that it
be granted the power Congress refused to give.

In 1957 the United States Commission on Government Security found that "[a]irplane journals, scientific periodi-
cals, and even the daily newspaper have featured articles
containing information and other data which should have
been deleted in whole or in part for security reasons." In
response to this problem the Commission proposed that

"Congress enact legislation making it a crime for any person willfully to disclose without proper authorization, for any purpose whatever, information classified 'secret' or 'top secret,' knowing, or having reasonable grounds to believe, such information to have been so classified." After substantial floor discussion on the proposal, it was rejected. If the proposal that Senator Cotton championed on the floor had been enacted, the publication of the documents involved here would certainly have been a crime. Congress refused, however, to make it a crime. The Government is here asking this Court to remake that decision. This Court has no such power.

Either the Government has the power under statutory grant to use traditional criminal law to protect the country or, if there is no basis for arguing that Congress has made the activity a crime, it is plain that Congress has specifically refused to grant the authority the Government seeks from this Court. In either case this Court does not have authority to grant the requested relief. It is not for this Court to fling itself into every breach perceived by some Government official nor is it for this Court to take on itself the burden of enacting law, especially a law that Congress has refused to pass. . . .

CHIEF JUSTICE WARREN BURGER, dissenting.

So clear are the constitutional limitations on prior restraint against expression, that from the time of *Near v. Minnesota* (1931) until recently in *Organization for a Better Austin v. Keefe* (1971), we have had little occasion to be concerned with cases involving prior restraints against news reporting on matters of public interest. There is, therefore, little variation among the members of the Court in terms of resistance to prior restraints against

publication. Adherence to this basic constitutional principle, however, does not make these cases simple. In these
cases, the imperative of a free and unfettered press comes
into collision with another imperative, the effective func-
tioning of a complex modern government and specifically
the effective exercise of certain constitutional powers of
the Executive. Only those who view the First Amendment as an absolute in all circumstances - a view I respect,
but reject - can find such cases as these to be simple or
easy.

These cases are not simple for another and more immediate reason. We do not know the facts of the cases. No
District Judge knew all the facts. No Court of Appeals
judge knew all the facts. No member of this Court knows
all the facts.

Why are we in this posture, in which only those judges to
whom the First Amendment is absolute and permits of no
restraint in any circumstances or for any reason, are really
in a position to act?

I suggest we are in this posture because these cases have
been conducted in unseemly haste. The prompt setting of
these cases reflects our universal abhorrence of prior restraint. But prompt judicial action does not mean unjudi-
cial haste.

Here, moreover, the frenetic haste is due in large part to
the manner in which the Times proceeded from the date it
obtained the purloined documents. It seems reasonably
clear now that the haste precluded reasonable and deliberate judicial treatment of these cases and was not warrant-
ed. The precipitate action of this Court aborting trials not

yet completed is not the kind of judicial conduct that ought to attend the disposition of a great issue.

The newspapers make a derivative claim [on behalf of others] under the First Amendment; they denominate [state] this right as the public "right to know"; by implication, the Times asserts a sole trusteeship of that right by virtue of its journalistic "scoop." The right is asserted as an absolute. Of course, the First Amendment right itself is not an absolute, as Justice Holmes so long ago pointed out in his aphorism concerning the right to shout "fire" in a crowded theater if there was no fire. There are other exceptions, some of which Chief Justice Hughes mentioned by way of example in *Near v. Minnesota.* There are no doubt other exceptions no one has had occasion to describe or discuss. Conceivably such exceptions may be lurking in these cases and would have been flushed had they been properly considered in the trial courts, free from unwarranted deadlines and frenetic pressures. An issue of this importance should be tried and heard in a judicial atmosphere conducive to thoughtful, reflective deliberation, especially when haste, in terms of hours, is unwarranted in light of the long period the Times, by its own choice, deferred publication.

It is not disputed that the Times has had unauthorized possession of the documents for three to four months, during which it has had its expert analysts studying them, presumably digesting them and preparing the material for publication. During all of this time, the Times, presumably in its capacity as trustee of the public's "right to know," has held up publication for purposes it considered proper and thus public knowledge was delayed. No doubt this was for a good reason; the analysis of 7,000 pages of complex material drawn from a vastly greater volume of material would inevitably take time and the writing of good news stories takes time. But why should the United States Government, from whom this information was illegally acquired by someone, along with all the counsel, trial judges, and appellate judges be placed under needless pressure? After these months of deferral, the alleged "right to know" has somehow and suddenly become a right that must be vindicated instant[ly].

Would it have been unreasonable, since the newspaper could anticipate the Government's objections to release of secret material, to give the Government an opportunity to review the entire collection and determine whether agreement could be reached on publication? Stolen or not, if security was not in fact jeopardized, much of the material could no doubt have been declassified, since it spans a period ending in 1968. With such an approach - one that great newspapers have in the past practiced and stated editorially to be the duty of an honorable press - the newspapers and Government might well have narrowed the area of disagreement as to what was and was not publishable, leaving the remainder to be resolved in orderly litigation, if necessary. To me it is hardly believable that a newspaper long regarded as a great institution in American life would fail to perform one of the basic and simple duties of every citizen with respect to the discovery or possession of stolen property or secret government documents. That duty, I had thought - perhaps naively - was to report forthwith, to responsible public officers. This duty rests on taxi drivers, Justices, and the New York Times. The course followed by the Times, whether so calculated or not, removed any possibility of orderly litigation of the issues. If the action of the judges up to now has been correct, that result is sheer happenstance.

Our grant of the writ of certiorari before final judgment in the *Times* case aborted the trial in the District Court before it had made a complete record pursuant to the mandate of the Court of Appeals for the Second Circuit.

The consequence of all this melancholy series of events is that we literally do not know what we are acting on. As I see it, we have been forced to deal with litigation concerning rights of great magnitude without an adequate record, and surely without time for adequate treatment either in the prior proceedings or in this Court. It is interesting to note that counsel on both sides, in oral argument before this Court, were frequently unable to respond to questions on factual points. Not surprisingly they pointed out that they had been working literally "around the clock" and simply were unable to review the documents that give rise to these cases and were not familiar with them. This Court is in no better posture.

I would affirm the Court of Appeals for the Second Circuit and allow the District Court to complete the trial aborted by our grant of certiorari, meanwhile preserving the status quo in the *Post* case. . . .

We all crave speedier judicial processes but when judges are pressured as in these cases the result is a parody of the judicial function.

ABORTION

ROE v. WADE

The Abortion Decision originates in Texas. "Jane Roe" a pregnant single woman brought an action in U.S. District Court against Wade, the District Attorney of Dallas County, challenging the constitutionality of the Texas abortion laws. The District Court found partially for Roe and both sides in the controversy appealed to the U.S. Supreme Court which granted a review.

Oral arguments were heard on December 13, 1971, the case was reargued on October 11, 1972 and a decision was announced on January 22, 1973.

Justice Harry Blackmun delivered the opinion of the Court. Chief Justice Warren Burger and Justices William Douglas and Potter Stewart issued concurring opinions. Justices Rehnquist and White issued dissenting opinions.

The complete text of *Roe v. Wade* can be found in United States Reports, volume 410, page 113.

ROE v. WADE

January 22, 1973

JUSTICE HARRY BLACKMUN: This Texas federal appeal ... present[s] constitutional challenges to state criminal abortion legislation. The Texas statutes under attack here are typical of those that have been in effect in many States for approximately a century.

We forthwith acknowledge our awareness of the sensitive and emotional nature of the abortion controversy, of the vigorous opposing views, even among physicians, and of the deep and seemingly absolute convictions that the subject inspires. One's philosophy, one's experiences, one's exposure to the raw edges of human existence, one's religious training, one's attitudes toward life and family and their values, and the moral standards one establishes and seeks to observe, are all likely to influence and to color one's thinking and conclusions about abortion.

In addition, population growth, pollution, poverty, and racial overtones tend to complicate and not to simplify the problem.

Our task, of course, is to resolve the issue by constitutional measurement, free of emotion and of predilection. We seek earnestly to do this, and, because we do, we have inquired into, and in this opinion place some emphasis upon, medical and medical-legal history and what that history reveals about man's attitudes toward the abortion procedure over the centuries. We bear in mind, too, Justice Holmes' admonition ... in *Lochner v. New York* (1905):

"[The Constitution] is made for people of
fundamentally differing views, and the acci-
dent of our finding certain opinions natural
and familiar or novel and even shocking
ought not to conclude our judgment upon
the question whether statutes embodying
them conflict with the Constitution of the
United States."

The Texas statutes that concern us here . . . make it a
crime to "procure an abortion," . . . or to attempt one, except with respect to "an abortion procured or attempted
by medical advice for the purpose of saving the life of the
mother." Similar statutes are in existence in a majority of
the States.

Texas first enacted a criminal abortion statute in 1854.
This was soon modified [in 1857, 1866, 1879, and 1911]
into language that has remained substantially unchanged
to the present time. The final article in each of these
compilations provided the same exception . . . for an abortion by "medical advice for the purpose of saving the life
of the mother."

Jane Roe [the name is a pseudonym], a single woman who
was residing in Dallas County, Texas, instituted this federal action in March 1970 against the District Attorney of
the county. She sought a declaratory judgment [a conclu-
sive, binding statement by the court] that the Texas criminal abortion statutes were unconstitutional . . . and an injunction [an order from the court] restraining
[preventing] the defendant [the District Attorney] from
enforcing the statutes.

Roe [claimed] that she was unmarried and pregnant; that she wished to terminate her pregnancy by an abortion "performed by a competent, licensed physician, under safe, clinical conditions"; that she was unable to get a "legal" abortion in Texas because her life did not appear to be threatened by the continuation of her pregnancy; and that she could not afford to travel to another jurisdiction in order to secure a legal abortion under safe conditions. She claimed that the Texas statutes were unconstitutionally vague and that they abridged her right of personal privacy, protected by the First, Fourth, Fifth, Ninth, and Fourteenth Amendments. By an amendment to her complaint Roe purported to sue "on behalf of herself and all other women" similarly situated.

Despite the use of the pseudonym, no suggestion is made that Roe is a fictitious person. For purposes of her case, we accept as true, and as established, her existence; her pregnant state, as of the inception of her suit in March 1970 and as late as May 21 of that year when she filed an alias affidavit with the District Court; and her inability to obtain a legal abortion in Texas.

Viewing Roe's case as of the time of its filing and thereafter until as late as May, there can be little dispute that it then presented a case or controversy and that . . . she, as a pregnant single woman thwarted by the Texas criminal abortion laws, had [the legal right] to challenge those statutes. . . .

[Wade] notes, however, that the record does not disclose that Roe was pregnant at the time of the District Court hearing on May 22, 1970, or on the following June 17 when the court's opinion and judgment were filed. And he suggests that Roe's case must now be moot [no longer

in controversy] because she . . . [is] no longer subject to
any 1970 pregnancy.

The usual rule in federal cases is that an actual controversy must exist at stages of appellate . . . review, and not
simply at the date the action is initiated.

But when, as here, pregnancy is a significant fact in the
litigation, the normal 266-day human gestation period is
so short that the pregnancy will come to term before the
usual appellate process is complete. If that termination
makes a case moot, pregnancy litigation seldom will survive much beyond the trial stage, and appellate review
will be effectively denied. Our law should not be that rigid. Pregnancy often comes more than once to the same
woman, and in the general population, if man is to survive, it will always be with us. Pregnancy provides a clas-
sic justification for a conclusion of nonmootness. It truly
could be "capable of repetition, yet evading review."

We, therefore, agree with the District Court that Jane Roe
had [the right] to undertake this litigation, that she presented a justiciable controversy, and that the termination
of her 1970 pregnancy has not rendered her case moot. . .

The principal thrust of appellant's attack on the Texas
statutes is that they improperly invade a right, said to be
possessed by the pregnant woman, to choose to terminate
her pregnancy. [Roe claims] this right in the concept of
personal "liberty" embodied in the Fourteenth Amendment's Due Process Clause; or in personal, marital, famili-
al, and sexual privacy said to be protected by the Bill of
Rights or its penumbras; or among those rights reserved
to the people by the Ninth Amendment. Before addressing this claim, we feel it desirable briefly to survey, in

several aspects, the history may afford us, and then to examine the state purposes and interests behind the criminal abortion laws.

It perhaps is not generally appreciated that the restrictive criminal abortion laws in effect in a majority of States today are of relatively recent vintage. Those laws, generally proscribing [prohibiting] abortion or its attempt at any time during pregnancy except when necessary to preserve the pregnant woman's life, are not of ancient or even of common-law origin. Instead, they derive from statutory [legislative] changes effected, for the most part, in the latter half of the 19th century.

1. *Ancient attitudes.* These are not capable of precise determination. We are told that at the time of the Persian Empire abortifacients were known and that criminal abortions were severely punished. We are also told, however, that abortion was practiced in Greek times as well as in the Roman Era, and that "it was resorted to without scruple." The Ephesian, Soranos, often described as the greatest of the ancient gynecologists, appears to have been generally opposed to Rome's prevailing free-abortion practices. He found it necessary to think first of the life of the mother, and he resorted to abortion when, upon this standard, he felt the procedure advisable. Greek and Roman law afforded little protection to the unborn. If abortion was prosecuted in some places, it seems to have been based on a concept of a violation of the father's right to his offspring. Ancient religion did not bar abortion.

2. *The Hippocratic Oath.* What then of the famous Oath that has stood so long as the ethical guide of the medical profession and that bears the name of the great Greek, who has been described as the Father of Medicine, the

"wisest and the greatest practitioner of his art," and the "most important and most complete medical personality of antiquity," who dominated the medical schools of his time, and who typified the sum of the medical knowledge of the past? The Oath varies somewhat according to the particular translation, but in any translation the content is clear: "I will give no deadly medicine to anyone if asked, nor suggest any such counsel; and in like manner I will not give to a woman a pessary to produce abortion," or "I will neither give a deadly drug to anybody if asked for it, nor will I make a suggestion to this effect. Similarly, I will not give to a woman an abortive remedy."

Although the Oath is not mentioned in any of the principal briefs in this case . . . , it represents the apex of the development of strict ethical concepts in medicine, and its influence endures to this day. Why did not the authority of Hippocrates dissuade abortion practice in his time and that of Rome? The late Dr. Edelstein provides us with a theory: The Oath was not uncontested even in Hippocrates' day; only the Pythagorean school of philosophers frowned upon the related act of suicide. Most Greek thinkers, on the other hand, commended abortion, at least prior to viability. For the Pythagoreans, however, it was a matter of dogma. For them the embryo was animate from the moment of conception, and abortion meant destruction of a living being. The abortion clause of the Oath, therefore, "echoes Pythagorean doctrines," and [i]n no other stratum of Greek opinion were such views held or proposed in the same spirit of uncompromising austerity."

Dr. Edelstein then concludes that the Oath originated in a group representing only a small segment of Greek opinion and that it certainly was not accepted by all ancient physicians. He points out that medical writings down to Galen

(A.D. 130-200) "give evidence of the violation of almost every one of its injunctions." But with the end of antiquity a decided change took place. Resistance against suicide and against abortion became common. The Oath came to be popular. The emerging teachings of Christianity were in agreement with the Pythagorean ethic. The Oath "became the nucleus of all medical ethics" and "was applauded as the embodiment of truth." Thus, suggests Dr. Edelstein, it is "a Pythagorean manifesto and not the expression of an absolute standard of medical conduct."

This, it seems to us, is a satisfactory and acceptable explanation of the Hippocratic Oath's apparent rigidity. It enables us to understand, in historical context, a long-accepted and revered statement of medical ethics.

3. *The common law.* It is undisputed that at common law [court decisions], abortion performed *before* "quickening" - the first recognizable movement of the fetus *in utero,* appearing usually from the 16th to the 18th week of pregnancy - was not an indictable offense. The absence of a common-law crime for pre-quickening abortion appears to have developed from a confluence of earlier philosophical, theological, and civil and canon law concepts of when life begins. These disciplines variously approached the question in terms of the point at which the embryo or fetus became "formed" or recognizably human, or in terms of when a "person" came into being, that is, infused with a "soul" or "animated." A loose consensus evolved in early English law that these events occurred at some point between conception and live birth. This was "mediate animation." Although Christian theology and the canon law came to fix the point of animation at 40 days for a male and 80 days for a female, a view that persisted until the 19th century, there was otherwise little agreement about

the precise time of formation or animation. There was agreement, however, that prior to this point the fetus was to be regarded as part of the mother, and its destruction, therefore, was not homicide. Due to continued uncertainty about the precise time when animation occurred, to the lack of any empirical basis for the 40-80-day view, and perhaps to Aquinas' definition of movement as one of the two first principles of life, Bracton focused upon quickening as the critical point. The significance of quickening was echoed by later common-law scholars and found its way into the received [accepted] common law in this country.

Whether abortion of a *quick* fetus was a felony at common law, or even a lesser crime, is still disputed. Bracton, writing early in the 13th century, thought it homicide. But the later and predominant view, following the great common-law scholars, has been that it was, at most, a lesser offense. In a frequently cited passage, Coke took the position that abortion of a woman "quick with childe" is "a great misprision [an undefined crime], and no murder." Blackstone followed, saying that while abortion after quickening had once been considered manslaughter (though not murder), "modern law" took a less severe view. A recent review of the common-law precedents argues, however, that those precedents contradict Coke and that even post-quickening abortion was never established as a common-law crime. This is of some importance because while most American courts ruled, in holding [actual decision] or dictum [observations made in the decision], that abortion of an unquickened fetus was not criminal under their received common law, others followed Coke in stating that abortion of a quick fetus was a "misprision," a term they translated to mean "misdemeanor." That their reliance on Coke on this aspect of the law was uncritical and, apparently in all the reported cases, dictum (due probably to the paucity of common-law prosecutions for post-quickening abortion), makes it now appear doubtful that abortion was ever firmly established as a common-law crime even with respect to the destruction of a quick fetus.

4. *The English statutory law.* England's first criminal abortion statute, Lord Ellenborough's Act, came in 1803. It made abortion of a quick fetus . . . a capital crime, but . . . it provided lesser penalties for the felony of abortion before quickening, and thus preserved the "quickening" distinction. This contrast was continued in the general revision of 1828. It disappeared, however, together with the death penalty, in 1837, and did not reappear in the Offenses Against the Person Act of 1861 that formed the core of English anti-abortion law until the liberalizing reforms of 1967. In 1929, the Infant Life (Preservation) Act came into being. Its emphasis was upon the destruction of "the life of a child capable of being born alive." It made a willful act performed with the necessary intent a felony. It contained a proviso that one was not to be found guilty of the offense "unless it is proved that the act which caused the death of the child was not done in good faith for the purpose only of preserving the life of the mother."

A seemingly notable development in the English law was the case of *Rex v. Bourne* (1939). This case apparently answered in the affirmative the question whether an abortion necessary to preserve the life of the pregnant woman was excepted from the criminal penalties of the 1861 Act. In his instructions to the jury, Judge Macnaghten referred to the 1929 Act, and observed that that Act related to "the case where a child is killed by a wilful act at the time when it is being delivered in the ordinary course of nature." He concluded that the 1861 Act's use of the word "unlawfully," imported the same meaning expressed by the specific proviso in the 1929 Act, even though there was no mention of preserving the mother's life in the 1861 Act. He then construed the phrase "preserving the life of the mother" broadly, that is, "in a reasonable sense," to include a serious and permanent threat to the mother's *health*, and instructed the jury to acquit Dr. Bourne if it found he had acted in a good-faith belief that the abortion was necessary for this purpose. The jury did acquit.

Recently, Parliament enacted a new abortion law. This is the Abortion Act of 1967. The Act permits a licensed physician to perform an abortion where two other licensed physicians agree (a) "that the continuance of the pregnancy would involve risk to the life of the pregnant woman, or of injury to the physical or mental health of the pregnant woman or any existing children of her family, greater than if the pregnancy were terminated," or (b) "that there is a substantial risk that if the child were born it would suffer from such physical or mental abnormalities as to be seriously handicapped." The Act also provides that, in making this determination, "account may be taken of the pregnant woman's actual or reasonably foreseeable environment." It also permits a physician, without the concurrence of others, to terminate a pregnancy where he is of the good-faith opinion that the abortion "is immediately necessary to save the life or to prevent grave permanent injury to the physical or mental health of the pregnant woman."

5. *The American law.* In this country, the law in effect in all but a few States until mid-19th century was the pre-existing English common law. Connecticut, the first State

to enact abortion legislation, adopted in 1821 that part of
Lord Ellenborough's Act that related to a woman "quick
with child." The death penalty was not imposed. Abortion before quickening was made a crime in that State
only in 1860. In 1828, New York enacted legislation that,
in two respects, was to serve as a model for early anti-
abortion statutes. First, while barring destruction of an
unquickened fetus as well as a quick fetus, it made the
former only a misdemeanor, but the latter second-degree
manslaughter. Second, it incorporated a concept of therapeutic abortion by providing that an abortion was excused
if it "shall have been necessary to preserve the life of such
mother, or shall have been advised by two physicians to be
necessary for such purpose." By 1840, when Texas had
received the common law, only eight American States had
statutes dealing with abortion. It was not until after the
War Between the States that legislation began generally to
replace the common law. Most of these initial statutes
dealt severely with abortion after quickening but were
lenient with it before quickening. Most punished attempts equally with completed abortions. While many
statutes included the exception for an abortion thought by
one or more physicians to be necessary to save the mother's life, that provision soon disappeared and the typical
law required that the procedure actually be necessary for
that purpose.

Gradually, in the middle and late 19th century the quickening distinction disappeared from the statutory law of
most States and the degree of the offense and the penalties were increased. By the end of the 1950's, a large majority of the jurisdictions banned abortion, however and
whenever performed, unless done to save or preserve the
life of the mother. The exceptions, Alabama and the District of Columbia, permitted abortion to preserve the

mother's health. Three States [Massachusetts, New Jersey, and Pennsylvania] permitted abortions that were not "unlawfully" performed or that were not "without lawful justification," leaving interpretation of those standards to the courts. In the past several years, however, a trend toward liberalization of abortion statutes has resulted in adoption, by about one-third of the States, of less stringent laws, most of them patterned after the ALI [American Law Institute]'s Model Penal Code....

It is thus apparent that at common law, at the time of the adoption of our Constitution, and throughout the major portion of the 19th century, abortion was viewed with less disfavor than under most American statutes currently in effect. Phrasing it another way, a woman enjoyed a substantially broader right to terminate a pregnancy than she does in most States today. At least with respect to the early stage of pregnancy, and very possibly without such a limitation, the opportunity to make this choice was present in this country well into the 19th century. Even later, the law continued for some time to treat less punitively an abortion procured in early pregnancy.

6. *The position of the American Medical Association.* The anti-abortion mood prevalent in this country in the late 19th century was shared by the medical profession. Indeed, the attitude of the profession may have played a significant role in the enactment of stringent criminal abortion legislation during that period.

An AMA Committee on Criminal Abortion was appointed in May 1857. It presented its report to the Twelfth Annual Meeting. That report observed that the Committee had been appointed to investigate criminal abortion "with a view to its general suppression." It deplored abortion and its frequency and it listed three causes of "this general demoralization":

> "The first of these causes is a wide-spread popular ignorance of the true character of the crime - a belief, even among mothers themselves, that the foetus is not alive till after the period of quickening.

> "The second of the agents alluded to is the fact that the profession themselves are frequently supposed careless of foetal life . . . .

> "The third reason of the frightful extent of this crime is found in the grave defects of our laws, both common and statute, as regards the independent and actual existence of the child before birth, as a living being. These errors, which are sufficient in most instances to prevent conviction, are based, and only based, upon mistaken and exploded medical dogmas. With strange inconsistency, the law fully acknowledges the foetus in utero and its inherent rights, for civil purposes; while personally and as criminally affected, it fails to recognize it, and to its life as yet denies all protection."

The Committee then offered, and the Association adopted, resolutions protesting "against such unwarrantable destruction of human life," calling upon state legislatures to revise their abortion laws, and requesting the cooperation of state medical societies "in pressing the subject."

In 1871 a long and vivid report was submitted by the
Committee on Criminal Abortion. It ended with the observation, "We had to deal with human life. In a matter
of less importance we could entertain no compromise. An
honest judge on the bench would call things by their
proper names. We could do no less." It profered resolutions, adopted by the Association recommending, among
other things, that it "be unlawful and unprofessional for
any physician to induce abortion or premature labor,
without the concurrent opinion of at least one respectable
consulting physician, and then always with a view to the
safety of the child - if that be possible," and calling "the
attention of the clergy of all denominations to the per-
verted views of morality entertained by a large class of
females - aye, and men also, on this important question."

Except for periodic condemnation of the criminal abor-
tionist, no further formal AMA action took place until
1967. In that year, the Committee on Human Reproduc-
tion urged the adoption of a stated policy of opposition to
induced abortion, except when there is "documented medical evidence" of a threat to the health or life of the mother, or that the child "may be born with incapacitating
physical deformity or mental deficiency," or that a pregnancy "resulting from legally established statutory or for-
cible rape or incest may constitute a threat to the mental
or physical health of the patient," two other physicians
"chosen because of their recognized professional competence have examined the patient and have concurred in
writing," and the procedure "is performed in a hospital accredited by the Joint Commission on Accreditation of
Hospitals." The providing of medical information by
physicians to state legislatures in their consideration of
legislation regarding therapeutic abortion was "to be considered consistent with the principles of ethics of the

American Medical Association." This recommendation was adopted by the House of Delegates.

In 1970, after the introduction of a variety of proposed resolutions, and of a report from its Board of Trustees, a reference committee noted "polarization of the medical profession on this controversial issue"; division among those who had testified; a difference of opinion among AMA councils and committees; "the remarkable shift in testimony" in six months, felt to be influenced "by the rapid changes in state laws and by the judicial decisions which tend to make abortion more freely available;"and a feeling "that this trend will continue." On June 25, 1970, the House of Delegates adopted preambles and most of the resolutions proposed by the reference committee. The preambles emphasized "the best interests of the patient," "sound clinical judgment," and "informed patient consent," in contrast to "mere acquiescence to the patient's demand." The resolutions asserted that abortion is a medical procedure that should be performed by a licensed physician in an accredited hospital only after consultation with two other physicians and in conformity with state law, and that no party to the procedure should be required to violate personally held moral principles. The AMA Judicial Council rendered a complementary opinion.

7. *The position of the American Public Health Association.* In October 1970, the Executive Board of the APHA adopted Standards for Abortion Services. These were five in number:

> "a. Rapid and simple abortion referral must
> be readily available through state and local
> public health departments, medical societies,
> or other non-profit organizations.

"b. An important function of counseling should be to simplify and expedite the provision of abortion services; it should not delay the obtaining of these services.

"c. Psychiatric consultation should not be mandatory. As in the case of other specialized medical services, psychiatric consultation should be sought for definite indications and not on a routine basis.

"d. A wide range of individuals from appropriately trained, sympathetic volunteers to highly skilled physicians may qualify as abortion counselors.

"e. Contraception and/or sterilization should be discussed with each abortion patient."

Among factors pertinent to life and health risks associated with abortion were three that "are recognized as important":

"a. the skill of the physician,

"b. the environment in which the abortion is performed, and above all

"c. the duration of pregnancy, as determined by uterine size and confirmed by menstrual history."

It was said that "a well-equipped hospital" offers more protection "to cope with unforeseen difficulties than an office or clinic without such resources. . . . The factor of gestational age is of overriding importance." Thus, it was recommended that abortions in the second trimester and early abortions in the presence of existing medical complications be performed in hospitals as in-patient procedures. For pregnancies in the first trimester, abortion in the hospital with or without overnight stay "is probably the safest practice." An abortion in an extramural facility, however, is an acceptable alternative "provided arrangements exist in advance to admit patients promptly if unforeseen complications develop." Standards for an abortion facility were listed. It was said that at present abortions should be performed by physicians or osteopaths who are licensed to practice and who have "adequate training."

8. *The position of the American Bar Association.* At its meeting in February 1972 the ABA House of Delegates approved, with 17 opposing votes, the Uniform Abortion Act that had been drafted and approved the preceding August by the Conference of Commissioners on Uniform State Laws.

Three reasons have been advanced to explain historically the enactment of criminal abortion laws in the 19th century and to justify their continued existence.

It has been argued occasionally that these laws were the product of a Victorian social concern to discourage illicit sexual conduct. Texas, however, does not advance this justification in the present case, and it appears that no court or commentator has taken the argument seriously. The appellants and *amici* [friends of the court] contend, moreover, that this is not a proper state purpose at all and suggest that, if it were, the Texas statutes are overbroad in protecting it since the law fails to distinguish between married and unwed mothers.

A second reason is concerned with abortion as a medical procedure. When most criminal abortion laws were first enacted, the procedure was a hazardous one for the woman. This was particularly true prior to the development of antisepsis. Antiseptic techniques, of course, were based on discoveries by Lister, Pasteur, and others first announced in 1867, but were not generally accepted and employed until about the turn of the century. Abortion mortality was high. Even after 1900, and perhaps until as late as the development of antibiotics in the 1940's, standard modern techniques such as dilation and curettage were not nearly so safe as they are today. Thus, it has been argued that a State's real concern in enacting a criminal abortion law was to protect the pregnant woman, that is, to restrain her from submitting to a procedure that placed her life in serious jeopardy.

Modern medical techniques have altered this situation. [Roe] . . . refer[s] to medical data indicating that abortion in early pregnancy, that is, prior to the end of the first trimester, although not without its risk, is now relatively safe. Mortality rates for women undergoing early abortions, where the procedure is legal, appear to be as low as or lower than the rates for normal childbirth. Consequently, any interest of the State in protecting the woman from an inherently hazardous procedure, except when it would be equally dangerous for her to forgo it, has largely disappeared. Of course, important state interests in the areas of health and medical standards do remain. The State has a legitimate interest in seeing to it that abortion, like any other medical procedure, is performed under circumstances that insure maximum safety for the patient. This interest obviously extends at least to the performing physician and his staff, to the facilities involved, to the availability of after-care, and to adequate provision for any complication or emergency that might arise. The prevalence of high mortality rates at illegal "abortion mills" strengthens, rather than weakens, the State's interest in regulating the conditions under which abortions are performed. Moreover, the risk to the woman increases as her pregnancy continues. Thus, the State retains a definite interest in protecting the woman's own health and safety when an abortion is proposed at a late stage of pregnancy.

The third reason is the State's interest - some phrase it in terms of duty - in protecting prenatal life. Some of the argument for this justification rests on the theory that a new human life is present from the moment of conception. The State's interest and general obligation to protect life then extends, it is argued, to prenatal life. Only when the life of the pregnant mother herself is at stake, balanced against the life she carries within her, should the interest of the embryo or fetus not prevail. Logically, of course, a legitimate state interest in this area need not stand or fall on acceptance of the belief that life begins at conception or at some other point prior to live birth. In assessing the State's interest, recognition may be given to the less rigid claim that as long as at least *potential* life is involved, the State may assert interests beyond the protection of the pregnant woman alone.

Parties challenging state abortion laws have sharply disputed in some courts the contention that a purpose of these laws, when enacted, was to protect prenatal life. Pointing to the absence of legislative history to support the contention, they claim that most state laws were designed solely to protect the woman. Because medical advances have lessened this concern, at least with respect to abortion in early pregnancy, they argue that with respect to such abortions the laws can no longer be justified by any state interest. There is some scholarly support for this view of original purpose. The few state courts called upon to interpret their laws in the late 19th and early 20th centuries did focus on the State's interest in protecting the woman's health rather than in preserving the embryo and fetus. Proponents of this view point out that in many States, including Texas, by statute or judicial interpretation, the pregnant woman herself could not be prosecuted for self-abortion or for cooperating in an abortion performed upon her by another. They claim that adoption of the "quickening" distinction through received common law and state statutes tacitly recognizes the greater health hazards inherent in late abortion and impliedly repudiates the theory that life begins at conception.

It is with these interests, and the weight to be attached to them, that this case is concerned.

The Constitution does not explicitly mention any right of privacy. In a line of decisions, however, going back perhaps as far as *Union Pacific R. Co. v. Botsford* (1891), the Court has recognized that a right of personal privacy, or a guarantee of certain areas or zones of privacy, does exist under the Constitution. In varying contexts, the Court or individual Justices have, indeed, found at least the roots of that right in the First Amendment; in the Fourth and Fifth Amendments; in the penumbras of the Bill of Rights; in the Ninth Amendment; or in the concept of liberty guaranteed by the first section of the Fourteenth Amendment. . . . [O]nly personal rights that can be deemed "fundamental" or "implicit in the concept of ordered liberty" are included in this guarantee of personal privacy. . . . [T]he right has some extension to activities relating to marriage; procreation; contraception; family relationships; and child rearing and education.

This right of privacy, whether it be founded in the Fourteenth Amendment's concept of personal liberty and restrictions upon state action, as we feel it is, or, as the District Court determined, in the Ninth Amendment's reservation of rights to the people, is broad enough to encompass a woman's decision whether or not to terminate her pregnancy. The detriment that the State would impose upon the pregnant woman by denying this choice altogether is apparent. Specific and direct harm medically diagnosable even in early pregnancy may be involved. Maternity, or additional offspring, may force upon the woman a distressful life and future. Psychological harm may be imminent. Mental and physical health may be taxed by child care. There is also the distress, for all concerned, associated with the unwanted child, and there is the problem of bringing a child into a family already unable, psychologically and otherwise, to care for it. In other cases, as in this one, the additional difficulties and continuing stigma of unwed motherhood may be involved. All these are factors the woman and her responsible physician necessarily will consider in consultation.

On the basis of elements such as these, appellant and some *amici* argue that the woman's right is absolute and that she is entitled to terminate her pregnancy at whatever time, in whatever way, and for whatever reason she alone chooses. With this we do not agree. [Roe]'s arguments that Texas either has no valid interest at all in regulating the abortion decision, or no interest strong enough to support any limitation upon the woman's sole determination, are unpersuasive. The Court's decisions recognizing a right of privacy also acknowledge that some state regulation in areas protected by that right is appropriate. As noted above, a State may properly assert important interests in safeguarding health, in maintaining medical standards, and in protecting potential life. At some point in pregnancy, these respective interests become sufficiently compelling to sustain regulation of the factors that govern the abortion decision. The privacy right involved, therefore, cannot be said to be absolute. In fact, it is not clear to us that the claim . . . that one has an unlimited right to do with one's body as one pleases bears a close relationship to the right of privacy previously articulated in the Court's decisions. The Court has refused to recognize an unlimited right of this kind in the past.

We, therefore, conclude that the right of personal privacy includes the abortion decision, but that this right is not unqualified and must be considered against important state interests in regulation.

We note that those federal and state courts that have recently considered abortion law challenges have reached the same conclusion. A majority, in addition to the District Court in the present case, have held state laws unconstitutional, at least in part, because of vagueness or because of overbreadth and abridgment of rights.

Others have sustained state statutes.

Although the results are divided, most of these courts have agreed that the right of privacy, however based, is broad enough to cover the abortion decision; that the right, nonetheless, is not absolute and is subject to some limitations; and that at some point the state interests as to protection of health, medical standards, and prenatal life, become dominant. We agree with this approach.

Where certain "fundamental rights" are involved, the Court has held that regulation limiting these rights may be justified only by a "compelling state interest," and that legislative enactments must be narrowly drawn to express only the legitimate state interests at stake.

In the recent abortion cases . . . courts have recognized these principles. Those striking down state laws have generally scrutinized the State's interests in protecting health and potential life, and have concluded that neither interest justified broad limitations on the reasons for which a physician and his pregnant patient might decide that she should have an abortion in the early stages of pregnancy. Courts sustaining [letting stand] state laws have held that the State's determinations to protect health or prenatal life are dominant and constitutionally justifiable.

The District Court held that [Wade] failed to meet his burden of demonstrating that the Texas statute's infringement upon Roe's rights was necessary to support a compelling state interest, and that, although [Wade] presented "several compelling justifications for state presence in the area of abortions," the statutes outstripped these justifications and swept "far beyond any areas of compelling state interest." [Roe] and [Wade] both contest that holding. [Roe], as has been indicated, claims an absolute right that bars any state imposition of criminal penalties in the area. [Wade] argues that the State's determination to recognize and protect prenatal life from and after conception constitutes a compelling state interest. As noted above, we do not agree fully with either formulation.

A. [Wade] and certain *amici* argue that the fetus is a "person" within the language and meaning of the Fourteenth Amendment. In support of this, they outline at length and in detail the well-known facts of fetal development. If this suggestion of personhood is established, [Roe]'s case, of course, collapses, for the fetus' right to life would then be guaranteed specifically by the Amendment. [Roe] conceded as much on reargument. On the other hand, [Wade] conceded on reargument that no case could be cited that holds that a fetus is a person within the meaning of the Fourteenth Amendment.

The Constitution does not define "person" in so many words. Section 1 of the Fourteenth Amendment contains three references to "person." The first, in defining "citizens," speaks of "persons born or naturalized in the United States." The word also appears both in the Due Process Clause and in the Equal Protection Clause. "Person" is used in other places in the Constitution: in the listing of qualifications for Representatives and Senators; in the Apportionment Clause; in the Migration and Importation provision; in the Emolument Clause; in the Electors provisions; in the provision outlining qualifications for the office of President; in the Extradition provisions; and in the Fifth, Twelfth, and Twenty-second Amendments, as well as in [Sections] 2 and 3 of the Fourteenth Amendment. But in nearly all these instances, the use of the word is such that it has application only postnatally. None indicates, with any assurance, that it has any possible pre-natal application.

All this, together with our observation that throughout the major portion of the 19th century prevailing legal abortion practices were far freer than they are today, persuades us that the word "person," as used in the Fourteenth Amendment, does not include the unborn. This is in accord with the results reached in those few cases where the issue has been squarely presented. Indeed, our

decision in *United States v. Vuitch* (1971) inferentially is
to the same effect, for we there would not have indulged
in statutory interpretation favorable to abortion in specified circumstances if the necessary consequence was the
termination of life entitled to Fourteenth Amendment
protection.

This conclusion, however, does not of itself fully answer
the contentions raised by Texas, and we pass on to other
considerations.

B. The pregnant woman cannot be isolated in her privacy.
She carries an embryo and, later, a fetus, if one accepts
the medical definitions of the developing young in the human uterus. The situation therefore is inherently different from marital intimacy, or bedroom possession of obscene material, or marriage, or procreation, or education. .
. . As we have intimated above, it is reasonable and appropriate for a State to decide that at some point in time
another interest, that of health of the mother or that of
potential human life, becomes significantly involved. The
woman's privacy is no longer sole and any right of privacy she possesses must be measured accordingly.

Texas urges that, apart from the Fourteenth Amendment,
life begins at conception and is present throughout pregnancy, and that, therefore, the State has a compelling interest in protecting that life from and after conception.
We need not resolve the difficult question of when life
begins. When those trained in the respective disciplines
of medicine, philosophy, and theology are unable to arrive
at any consensus, the judiciary, at this point in the development of man's knowledge, is not in a position to specu-
late as to the answer.

It should be sufficient to note briefly the wide divergence of thinking on this most sensitive and difficult question. There has always been strong support for the view that life does not begin until live birth. This was the belief of the Stoics. It appears to be the predominant, though not the unanimous, attitude of the Jewish faith. It may be taken to represent also the position of a large segment of the Protestant community, insofar as that can be ascertained; organized groups that have taken a formal position on the abortion issue have generally regarded abortion as a matter for the conscience of the individual and her family. As we have noted, the common law found greater significance in quickening. Physicians and their scientific colleagues have regarded that event with less interest and have tended to focus either upon conception, upon live birth, or upon the interim point at which the fetus becomes "viable," that is, potentially able to live outside the mother's womb, albeit with artificial aid. Viability is usually placed at about seven months (28 weeks) but may occur earlier, even at 24 weeks. The Aristotelian theory of "mediate animation," that held sway throughout the Middle Ages and the Renaissance in Europe, continued to be official Roman Catholic dogma until the 19th century, despite opposition to this "ensoulment" theory from those in the Church who would recognize the existence of life from the moment of conception. The latter is now, of course, the official belief of the Catholic Church. As one brief *amicus* discloses, this is a view strongly held by many non-Catholics as well, and by many physicians. Substantial problems for precise definition of this view are posed, however, by new embryological data that purport to indicate that conception is a "process" over time, rather than an event, and by new medical techniques such as menstrual extraction, the "morning-after" pill, implantation of embryos, artificial insemination, and even artificial wombs.

In areas other than criminal abortion, the law has been reluctant to endorse any theory that life, as we recognize it, begins before live birth or to accord legal rights to the unborn except in narrowly defined situations and except when the rights are contingent upon live birth. For example, the traditional rule of tort law denied recovery for prenatal injuries even though the child was born alive. That rule has been changed in almost every jurisdiction. In most States, recovery is said to be permitted only if the fetus was viable, or at least quick, when the injuries were sustained, though few courts have squarely so held. In a recent development, generally opposed by the commentators, some States permit the parents of a stillborn child to maintain an action for wrongful death because of prenatal injuries. Such an action, however, would appear to be one to vindicate the parents' interest and is thus consistent with the view that the fetus, at most, represents only the potentiality of life. Similarly, unborn children have been recognized as acquiring rights or interests by way of inheritance or other devolution of property, and have been represented by [legal representatives]. Perfection of the interests involved, again, has generally been contingent upon live birth. In short, the unborn have never been recognized in the law as persons in the whole sense.

In view of all this, we do not agree that, by adopting one theory of life, Texas may override the rights of the pregnant woman that are at stake. We repeat, however, that the State does have an important and legitimate interest in preserving and protecting the health of the pregnant woman, whether she be a resident of the State or a nonresident who seeks medical consultation and treatment there, and that it has still *another* important and legitimate interest in protecting the potentiality of human life. These interests are separate and distinct. Each grows in substantiality as the woman approaches term and, at a point during pregnancy, each becomes "compelling."

With respect to the State's important and legitimate interest in the health of the mother, the "compelling" point, in the light of present medical knowledge, is at approximately the end of the first trimester. This is so because of the now-established medical fact that until the end of the first trimester mortality in abortion may be less than mortality in normal childbirth. It follows that, from and after this point, a State may regulate the abortion procedure to the extent that the regulation reasonably relates to the preservation and protection of maternal health. Examples of permissible state regulation in this area are requirements as to the qualifications of the person who is to perform the abortion; as to the licensure of that person; as to the facility in which the procedure is to be performed, that is, whether it must be a hospital or may be a clinic or some other place of less-than-hospital status; as to the licensing of the facility; and the like.

This means, on the other hand, that, for the period of pregnancy prior to this "compelling" point, the attending physician, in consultation with his patient, is free to determine, without regulation by the State, that, in his medical judgment, the patient's pregnancy should be terminated. If that decision is reached, the judgment may be effectuated by an abortion free of interference by the State.

With respect to the State's important and legitimate interest in potential life, the "compelling" point is at viability. This is so because the fetus then presumably has the capability of meaningful life outside the mother's womb. State regulation protective of fetal life after viability thus has both logical and biological justifications. If the State is interested in protecting fetal life after viability, it may go so far as to proscribe [prohibit] abortion during that period, except when it is necessary to preserve the life or health of the mother.

Measured against these standards, [Article] 1196 of the Texas Penal Code, in restricting legal abortions to those "procured or attempted by medical advice for the purpose of saving the life of the mother," sweeps too broadly. The statute makes no distinction between abortions performed early in pregnancy and those performed later, and it limits to a single reason, "saving" the mother's life, the legal justification for the procedure. The statute, therefore, cannot survive the constitutional attack made upon it here. . .

To summarize and to repeat:

1. A state criminal abortion statute of the current Texas type, that excepts from criminality only a *lifesaving* procedure on behalf of the mother, without regard to pregnancy stage and without recognition of the other interests involved, is violative of the Due Process Clause of the Fourteenth Amendment.

> (a) For the stage prior to approximately the end of the first trimester, the abortion decision and its effectuation must be left to the medical judgment of the pregnant woman's attending physician.

> (b) For the stage subsequent to approximately the end of the first trimester, the

State, in promoting its interest in the health of the mother, may, if it chooses, regulate the abortion procedure in ways that are reasonably related to maternal health.

(c) For the stage subsequent to viability, the State in promoting its interest in the potentiality of human life may, if it chooses, regulate, and even proscribe, abortion except where it is necessary, in appropriate medical judgment, for the preservation of the life or health of the mother.

2. The State may define the term "physician" . . . to mean only a physician currently licensed by the State, and may proscribe any abortion by a person who is not a physician as so defined. . . .

This holding, we feel, is consistent with the relative weights of the respective interests involved, with the lessons and examples of medical and legal history, with the lenity of the common law, and with the demands of the profound problems of the present day. The decision leaves the State free to place increasing restrictions on abortion as the period of pregnancy lengthens, so long as those restrictions are tailored to the recognized state interests. The decision vindicates the right of the physician to administer medical treatment according to his professional judgment up to the points where important state interests provide compelling justifications for intervention. Up to those points, the abortion decision in all its aspects is inherently, and primarily, a medical decision, and basic responsibility for it must rest with the physician. If an individual practitioner abuses the privilege of exercising proper medical judgment, the usual remedies, judicial and intra-professional, are available.

Our conclusion that [Article] 1196 is unconstitutional means, of course, that the Texas abortion statutes, as a unit, must fall. . . .

JUSTICE WILLIAM REHNQUIST, dissenting: The Court's opinion brings to the decision of this troubling question both extensive historical fact and a wealth of legal scholarship. While the opinion thus commands my respect, I find myself nonetheless in fundamental disagreement with those parts of it that invalidate the Texas statute in question, and therefore dissent.

The Court's opinion decides that a State may impose virtually no restriction on the performance of abortions during the first trimester of pregnancy. Our previous decisions indicate that a necessary predicate for such an opinion is a plaintiff who was in her first trimester of pregnancy at some time during the pendency of her lawsuit. While a party may vindicate his own constitutional rights, he may not seek vindication for the rights of others. The Court's statement of facts in this case makes clear, however, that the record in no way indicates the presence of such a plaintiff. We know only that plaintiff Roe at the time of filing her complaint was a pregnant woman; for aught that appears in this record, she may have been in her *last* trimester of pregnancy as of the date the complaint was filed.

Nothing in the Court's opinion indicates that Texas might not constitutionally apply its proscription of abortion as written to a woman in that stage of pregnancy. Nonetheless, the Court uses her complaint against the Texas stat-

ute as a fulcrum for deciding that States may impose virtually no restrictions on medical abortions performed during the *first* trimester of pregnancy. In deciding such a
hypothetical lawsuit, the Court departs from the long-
standing admonition that it should never "formulate a rule
of constitutional law broader than is required by the precise facts to which it is to be applied."

Even if there were a plaintiff in this case capable of liti-
gating the issue which the Court decides, I would reach a
conclusion opposite to that reached by the Court. I have
difficulty in concluding, as the Court does, that the right
of "privacy" is involved in this case. Texas, by the statute
here challenged, bars the performance of a medical abortion by a licensed physician on a plaintiff such as Roe. A
transaction resulting in an operation such as this is not
"private" in the ordinary usage of that word. Nor is the
"privacy" that the Court finds here even a distant relative
of the freedom from searches and seizures protected by
the Fourth Amendment to the Constitution, which the
Court has referred to as embodying a right to privacy.

If the Court means by the term "privacy" no more than
that the claim of a person to be free from unwanted state
regulation of consensual transactions may be a form of
"liberty" protected by the Fourteenth Amendment, there
is no doubt that similar claims have been upheld in our
earlier decisions on the basis of that liberty. I agree with
the statement of Justice Stewart in his concurring opinion
[not included in this book] that the "liberty," against deprivation of which without due process the Fourteenth
Amendment protects, embraces more than the rights
found in the Bill of Rights. But that liberty is not guaranteed absolutely against deprivation, only against deprivation without due process of law. The test traditionally ap-

plied in the area of social and economic legislation is whether or not a law such as that challenged has a rational relation to a valid state objective. The Due Process Clause of the Fourteenth Amendment undoubtedly does place a limit, albeit a broad one, on legislative power to enact laws such as this. If the Texas statute were to prohibit an abortion even where the mother's life is in jeopardy, I have little doubt that such a statute would lack a rational relation to a valid state objective under the test stated in *Williamson*. But the Court's sweeping invalidation of any restrictions on abortion during the first trimester is impossible to justify under that standard, and the conscious weighing of competing factors that the Court's opinion apparently substitutes for the established test is far more appropriate to a legislative judgment than to a judicial one.

The Court eschews the history of the Fourteenth Amendment in its reliance on the "compelling state interest" test. But the Court adds a new wrinkle to this test by transposing it from the legal considerations associated with the Equal Protection Clause of the Fourteenth Amendment to this case arising under the Due Process Clause of the Fourteenth Amendment. Unless I misapprehend the consequences of this transplanting of the "compelling state interest test," the Court's opinion will accomplish the seemingly impossible feat of leaving this area of the law more confused than it found it.

While the Court's opinion quotes from the dissent of Justice Holmes in *Lochner v. New York*, the result it reaches is more closely attuned to the majority opinion of Justice Peckham in that case. As in *Lochner* and similar cases applying substantive due process standards to economic and social welfare legislation, the adoption of the compelling state interest standard will inevitably require this Court to

examine the legislative policies and pass on the wisdom of
these policies in the very process of deciding whether a
particular state interest put forward may or may not be
"compelling." The decision here to break pregnancy into
three distinct terms and to outline the permissible restrictions the State may impose in each one, for example, par-
takes more of judicial legislation than it does of a determination of the intent of the drafters of the Fourteenth
Amendment.

The fact that a majority of the States reflecting, after all,
the majority sentiment in those States, have had restrictions on abortions for at least a century is a strong indication, it seems to me, that the asserted right to an abortion
is not "so rooted in the traditions and conscience of our
people as to be ranked as fundamental." Even today,
when society's views on abortion are changing, the very
existence of the debate is evidence that the "right" to an
abortion is not so universally accepted as [Roe] would
have us believe.

To reach its result, the Court necessarily has had to find
within the scope of the Fourteenth Amendment a right
that was apparently completely unknown to the drafters
of the Amendment. As early as 1821, the first state law
dealing directly with abortion was enacted by the Connecticut Legislature. By the time of the adoption of the
Fourteenth Amendment in 1868, there were at least 36
laws enacted by state or territorial legislatures limiting
abortion. While many States have amended or updated
their laws, 21 of the laws on the books in 1868 remain in
effect today. Indeed, the Texas statute struck down today
was, as the majority notes, first enacted in 1857 and "has
remained substantially unchanged to the present time."

There apparently was no question concerning the validity of this provision or of any of the other state statutes when the Fourteenth Amendment was adopted. The only conclusion possible from this history is that the drafters did not intend to have the Fourteenth Amendment withdraw from the States the power to legislate with respect to this matter.

Even if one were to agree that the case that the Court decides were here, and that the enunciation of the substantive constitutional law in the Court's opinion were proper, the actual disposition of the case by the Court is still difficult to justify. The Texas statute is struck down *in toto*, even though the Court apparently concedes that at later periods of pregnancy Texas might impose these selfsame statutory limitations on abortion. My understanding of past practice is that a statute found to be invalid as applied to a particular plaintiff, but not unconstitutional as a whole, is not simply "struck down" but is, instead, declared unconstitutional as applied to the fact situation before the Court.

For all of the foregoing reasons, I respectfully dissent.

AFFIRMATIVE ACTION

UNIVERSITY OF CALIFORNIA v. BAKKE

The Bakke Decision originates in California. Allan Bakke, a white male, applied twice, and was denied admission twice, to a University of California Medical School despite test scores superior to minority applicants who were accepted to the University under its special admissions program. Bakke filed suit in the Superior Court of California, requesting the Court order his admission and claiming that the University's special admissions program excluded him on the basis of his race, a violation of the Equal Protection Clause of the Fourteenth Amendment, the California Constitution and the Civil Rights Act of 1964.

The trial court found that the University's admission program violated the laws of the United States and California. The Court however refused to order Bakke's admission. Bakke appealed the part of the decision denying him admission. The University appealed the part of the decision finding its special admission program unlawful. The Supreme Court of California granted a review, affirmed the decision on the University's special admissions program and ordered that Bakke be admitted. The University appealed to the United States Supreme Court which granted a review.

Oral arguments were heard October 12, 1977 and the decision of the Court was announced June 28, 1978.

The decision of the court was delivered by Justice Lewis Powell. Chief Justice Earl Warren and Justices William Brennan, Byron White, Thurgood Marshall, Harry Blackmun, John Paul Stevens, Potter Stewart, and William Rehnquist concurred in part and dissented in part.

The complete text of *University of California v. Bakke* can be found in United States Reports, volume 438, page 265.

UNIVERSITY OF CALIFORNIA v. BAKKE

June 28, 1978

JUSTICE LEWIS POWELL: This case presents a challenge to the special admissions program of the petitioner, the Medical School of the University of California at Davis, which is designed to assure the admission of a specified number of students from certain minority groups. The Superior Court of California sustained respondent [Bakke]'s challenge, holding that petitioner's program violated the California Constitution, Title VI of the Civil Rights Act of 1964, and the Equal Protection Clause of the Fourteenth Amendment. The court enjoined petitioner [prevented the University] from considering [Bakke]'s race or the race of any other applicant in making admissions decisions. It refused, however, to order [Bakke]'s admission to the Medical School, holding that he had not carried his burden of proving that he would have been admitted but for the constitutional and statutory violations. The Supreme Court of California affirmed [let stand] those portions of the trial court's judgment declaring the special admissions program unlawful and [prevented the University] from considering the race of any applicant. It . . . directed the trial court to order [Bakke's] admission.

The Medical School of the University of California at Davis opened in 1968 with an entering class of 50 students. In 1971, the size of the entering class was increased to 100 students, a level at which it remains. No admissions program for disadvantaged or minority students existed when the school opened, and the first class contained three Asians but no blacks, no Mexican-Americans, and no American Indians. Over the next two years, the faculty devised a special admissions program to increase the rep-

resentation of "disadvantaged" students in each Medical
School class. The special program consisted of a separate
admissions system operating in coordination with the regular admissions process.

Under the regular admissions procedure, a candidate could
submit his application to the Medical School beginning in
July of the year preceding the academic year for which
admission was sought. Because of the large number of applications, the admissions committee screened each one to
select candidates for further consideration. Candidates
whose overall undergraduate grade point averages fell below 2.5 on a scale of 4.0 were summarily rejected. About
one out of six applicants was invited for a personal interview. Following the interviews, each candidate was rated
on a scale of 1 to 100 by his interviewers and four other
members of the admissions committee. The rating embraced the interviewers' summaries, the candidate's overall grade point average, grade point average in science
courses, scores on the Medical College Admissions Test
(MCAT), letters of recommendation, extracurricular activities, and other biographical data. The ratings were added
together to arrive at each candidate's "benchmark" score.
Since five committee members rated each candidate in
1973, a perfect score was 500; in 1974, six members rated
each candidate, so that a perfect score was 600. The full
committee then reviewed the file and scores of each applicant and made offers of admission on a "rolling" basis.
The chairman was responsible for placing names on the
waiting list. They were not placed in strict numerical order; instead, the chairman had discretion to include persons with "special skills."

The special admissions program operated with a separate
committee, a majority of whom were members of minori-

ty groups. On the 1973 application form, candidates were asked to indicate whether they wished to be considered as "economically and/or educationally disadvantaged" applicants; on the 1974 form the question was whether they wished to be considered as members of a "minority group," which the Medical School apparently viewed as "Blacks," "Chicanos," "Asians," and "American Indians." If these questions were answered affirmatively, the application was forwarded to the special admission committee. No formal definition of "disadvantaged" was ever produced, but the chairman of the special committee screened each application to see whether it reflected economic or educational deprivation. Having passed this initial hurdle, the applications then were rated by the special committee in a fashion similar to that used by the general admissions committee, except that special candidates did not have to meet the 2.5 grade point average cutoff applied to regular applicants. About one-fifth of the total number of special applicants were invited for interviews in 1973 and 1974. Following each interview, the special committee assigned each special applicant a benchmark score. The special committee then presented its top choices to the general admissions committee. The latter did not rate or compare the special candidates against the general applicants, but could reject recommended special candidates for failure to meet course requirements or other specific deficiencies. The special committee continued to recommend special applicants until a number prescribed by faculty vote were admitted. While the overall class size was still 50, the prescribed number was 8; in 1973 and 1974, when the class size had doubled to 100, the prescribed number of special admissions also doubled, to 16.

From the year of the increase in class size - 1971 - through 1974, the special program resulted in the admission of 21 black students, 30 Mexican-Americans, and 12 Asians, for a total of 63 minority students. Over the same period, the regular admissions program produced 1 black, 6 Mexican-Americans, and 37 Asians, for a total of 44 minority students. Although disadvantaged whites applied to the special program in large numbers, none received an offer of admission through that process. Indeed, in 1974, the special committee explicitly considered only "disadvantaged" special applicants who were members of one of the designated minority groups.

Allan Bakke is a white male who applied to the Davis Medical School in both 1973 and 1974. In both years Bakke's application was considered under the general admissions program, and he received an interview. His 1973 interview was with Dr. Theodore C. West, who considered Bakke "a very desirable applicant to [the] medical school." Despite a strong benchmark score of 468 out of 500, Bakke was rejected. His application had come late in the year, and no applicants in the general admissions process with scores below 470 were accepted after Bakke's application was completed. There were four special admissions slots unfilled at that time, however, for which Bakke was not considered. After his 1973 rejection, Bakke wrote to Dr. George H. Lowrey, Associate Dean and Chairman of the Admissions Committee, protesting that the special admissions program operated as a racial and ethnic quota.

Bakke's 1974 application was completed early in the year. His student interviewer gave him an overall rating of 94, finding him "friendly, well tempered, conscientious and delightful to speak with." His faculty interviewer was, by coincidence, the same Dr. Lowrey to whom he had written in protest of the special admissions program. Dr. Lowrey found Bakke "rather limited in his approach" to the problems of the medical profession and found disturbing Bakke's "very definite opinions which were based more on his personal viewpoints than upon a study of the total problem." Dr. Lowrey gave Bakke the lowest of his six ratings, an 86; his total was 549 out of 600. Again, Bakke's application was rejected. In neither year did the chairman of the admissions committee, Dr. Lowrey, exercise his discretion to place Bakke on the waiting list. In both years, applicants were admitted under the special program with grade point averages, MCAT scores, and benchmark scores significantly lower than Bakke's.

After the second rejection, Bakke filed . . . suit in the Superior Court of California. He sought . . . relief compelling his admission to the Medical School. He alleged that the Medical School's special admissions program operated to exclude him from the school on the basis of his race, in violation of his rights under the Equal Protection Clause of the Fourteenth Amendment . . . the California Constitution, and . . . Title VI of the Civil Rights Act of 1964. The University cross-complained for a declaration that its special admissions program was lawful. The trial court found that the special program operated as a racial quota, because minority applicants in the special program were rated only against one another, and 16 places in the class of 100 were reserved for them. Declaring that the University could not take race into account in making admissions decisions, the trial court held the challenged program violative of the Federal Constitution, the State Constitution, and Title VI. The court refused to order Bakke's admission, however, holding that he had failed to carry his burden of proving that he would have been admitted but for the existence of the special program.

Bakke appealed from the portion of the trial court judgment denying him admission, and the University appealed from the decision that its special admissions program was unlawful and the order enjoining [stopping] it from considering race in the processing of applications. The Supreme Court of California transferred the case directly from the trial court, "because of the importance of the issues involved." The California court accepted the findings of the trial court with respect to the University's program. Because the special admissions program involved a racial classification, the Supreme Court held itself bound to apply strict scrutiny. It then turned to the goals the University presented as justifying the special program. Although the court agreed that the goals of integrating the medical profession and increasing the number of physicians willing to serve members of minority groups were compelling state interests, it concluded that the special admissions program was not the least intrusive means of achieving those goals. Without passing on the state constitutional or the federal statutory grounds cited in the trial court's judgment, the California court held that the Equal Protection Clause of the Fourteenth Amendment required that "no applicant may be rejected because of his race, in favor of another who is less qualified, as measured by standards applied without regard to race."

Turning to Bakke's appeal, the court ruled that since Bakke had established that the University had discriminated against him on the basis of his race, the burden of proof shifted to the University to demonstrate that he would not have been admitted even in the absence of the special admissions program. The court analogized Bakke's situation to that of a plaintiff under Title VII of the Civil Rights Act of 1964. On this basis, the court initially ordered a remand [return to the lower court] for the purpose of determining whether, under the newly allocated burden of proof, Bakke would have been admitted to either the 1973 or the 1974 entering class in the absence of the special admissions program. In its petition for rehearing below, however, the University conceded its inability to carry that burden. The California court thereupon amended its opinion to direct that the trial court enter judgment ordering Bakke's admission to the Medical School. That order was stayed pending review in this Court. We granted [review] to consider the important constitutional issue. . . .

The language of [Section] 601 [of the Civil Rights Act of 1967], like that of the Equal Protection Clause, is majestic in its sweep:

> "No person in the United States shall, on the ground of race, color, or national origin, be excluded from participation in, be denied the benefits of, or be subjected to discrimination under any program or activity receiving Federal financial assistance."

The concept of "discrimination," like the phrase "equal protection of the laws," is susceptible of varying interpretations, for as Justice Holmes declared, "[a] word is not a crystal, transparent and unchanged, it is the skin of a living thought and may vary greatly in color and content according to the circumstances and the time in which it is used." We must, therefore, seek whatever aid is available in determining the precise meaning of the statute before us. Examination of the voluminous legislative history of Title VI reveals a congressional intent to halt federal funding of entities that violate a prohibition of racial discrimination similar to that of the Constitution. Although isolated statements of various legislators, taken out of context, can be marshaled in support of the proposition that [Section] 601 enacted a purely colorblind scheme, without regard to the reach of the Equal Protection Clause, these comments must be read against the background of both the problem that Congress was addressing and the broader view of the statute that emerges from a full examination of the legislative debates.

The problem confronting Congress was discrimination against Negro citizens at the hands of recipients of federal moneys. Indeed, the colorblindness pronouncements . . . generally occur in the midst of extended remarks dealing with the evils of segregation in federally funded programs. Over and over again, proponents of the bill detailed the plight of Negroes seeking equal treatment in such programs. There simply was no reason for Congress to consider the validity of hypothetical preferences that might be accorded minority citizens; the legislators were dealing with the real and pressing problem of how to guarantee those citizens equal treatment.

In addressing that problem, supporters of Title VI repeatedly declared that the bill enacted constitutional principles. For example, Representative Celler, the Chairman of the House Judiciary Committee and floor manager of the legislation in the House, emphasized this in introducing the bill:

"The bill would offer assurance that hospitals financed by Federal money would not deny adequate care to Negroes. It would prevent abuse of food distribution programs whereby Negroes have been known to be denied food surplus supplies when white persons were given such food. It would assure Negroes the benefits now accorded only white students in programs of high[er] education financed by Federal funds. It would, in short, *assure the existing right to equal treatment* in the enjoyment of Federal funds. It would not destroy any rights of private property or freedom of association."

Other sponsors shared Representative Celler's view that Title VI embodied constitutional principles.

In the Senate, Senator Humphrey declared that the purpose of Title VI was "to insure that Federal funds are spent in accordance with the Constitution and the moral sense of the Nation." Senator Ribicoff agreed that Title VI embraced the constitutional standard: "Basically, there is a constitutional restriction against discrimination in the use of federal funds; and Title VI simply spells out the procedure to be used in enforcing that restriction." Other Senators expressed similar views.

Further evidence of the incorporation of a constitutional standard into Title VI appears in the repeated refusals of the legislation's supporters precisely to define the term "discrimination. Opponents sharply criticized this failure, but proponents of the bill merely replied that the meaning of "discrimination" would be made clear by reference to the Constitution or other existing law. For example, Senator Humphrey noted the relevance of the Constitution:

> "As I have said, the bill has a simple purpose. That purpose is to give fellow citizens - Negroes - the same rights and opportunities that white people take for granted. This is no more than what was preached by the prophets, and by Christ Himself. It is

no more than what our Constitution guarantees."

In view of the clear legislative intent, Title VI must be
held to proscribe only those racial classifications that
would violate the Equal Protection Clause or the Fifth
Amendment.

[The University] does not deny that decisions based on
race or ethnic origin by faculties and administrations of
state universities are reviewable under the Fourteenth
Amendment. For his part, [Bakke] does not argue that all
racial or ethnic classifications are *per se* [inherently] invalid. The parties do disagree as to the level of judicial
scrutiny to be applied to the special admissions program.
[The University] argues that the court below erred in applying strict scrutiny, as this inexact term has been applied in our cases. That level of review, [the University]
asserts, should be reserved for classifications that disadvantage "discrete and insular minorities." [Bakke], on the
other hand, contends that the California court correctly
rejected the notion that the degree of judicial scrutiny accorded a particular racial or ethnic classification hinges
upon membership in a discrete and insular minority and
duly recognized that the "rights established [by the Fourteenth Amendment] are personal rights."

En route to this crucial battle over the scope of judicial
review, the parties fight a sharp preliminary action over
the proper characterization of the special admissions program. [The University] prefers to view it as establishing a
"goal" of minority representation in the Medical School.
[Bakke], echoing the courts below, labels it a racial quota.

This semantic distinction is beside the point: The special admissions program is undeniably a classification based on race and ethnic background. To the extent that there existed a pool of at least minimally qualified minority applicants to fill the 16 special admissions seats, white applicants could compete only for 84 seats in the entering class, rather than the 100 open to minority applicants. Whether this limitation is described as a quota or a goal, it is a line drawn on the basis of race and ethnic status.

The guarantees of the Fourteenth Amendment extend to all persons. Its language is explicit: "No State shall . . . deny to any person within its jurisdiction the equal protection of the laws." It is settled beyond question that the "rights created by the first section of the Fourteenth Amendment are, by its terms, guaranteed to the individual. The rights established are personal rights." The guarantee of equal protection cannot mean one thing when applied to one individual and something else when applied to a person of another color. If both are not accorded the same protection, then it is not equal.

Nevertheless, petitioner argues that the court below erred in applying strict scrutiny to the special admissions program because white males, such as respondent, are not a "discrete and insular minority" requiring extraordinary protection from the majoritarian political process. This rationale, however, has never been invoked in our decisions as a prerequisite to subjecting racial or ethnic distinctions to strict scrutiny. Nor has this Court held that discreteness and insularity constitute necessary preconditions to a holding that a particular classification is invidious. These characteristics may be relevant in deciding whether or not to add new types of classifications to the list of "suspect" categories or whether a particular classification survives close examination. Racial and ethnic classifications, however, are subject to stringent examination without regard to these additional characteristics. We declared as much in the first cases explicitly to recognize racial distinctions as suspect:

> "Distinctions between citizens solely because of their ancestry are by their very nature odious to a free people whose institutions are founded upon the doctrine of equality."

> "[A]ll legal restrictions which curtail the civil rights of a single racial group are immediately suspect. That is not to say that all such restrictions are unconstitutional. It is to say that courts must subject them to the most rigid scrutiny."

The Court has never questioned the validity of those pronouncements. Racial and ethnic distinctions of any sort are inherently suspect and thus call for the most exacting judicial examination.

This perception of racial and ethnic distinctions is rooted in our Nation's constitutional and demographic history. The Court's initial view of the Fourteenth Amendment was that its "one pervading purpose" was "the freedom of the slave race, the security and firm establishment of that freedom, and the protection of the newly-made freeman and citizen from the oppressions of those who had formerly exercised dominion over him." The Equal Protection Clause, however, was "[v]irtually strangled in infancy by post-civil-war judicial reactionism." It was relegated to decades of relative [disuse] while the Due Process Clause of the Fourteenth Amendment, after a short germinal period, flourished as a cornerstone in the Court's defense of property and liberty of contract. In that cause, the Fourteenth Amendment's "one pervading purpose" was displaced. It was only as the era of substantive due process came to a close that the Equal Protection Clause began to attain a genuine measure of vitality.

By that time it was no longer possible to peg the guarantees of the Fourteenth Amendment to the struggle for equality of one racial minority. During the dormancy of the Equal Protection Clause, the United States had become a Nation of minorities. Each had to struggle - and to some extent struggles still - to overcome the prejudices not of a monolithic majority, but of a "majority" composed of various minority groups of whom it was said - perhaps unfairly in many cases - that a shared characteristic was a willingness to disadvantage other groups. As the Nation filled with the stock of many lands, the reach of the Clause was gradually extended to all ethnic groups seeking protection from official discrimination. The guarantees of equal protection, said the Court in *Yick Wo*, "are universal in their application, to all persons within the territorial jurisdiction, without regard to any differences of race, of color, or of nationality; and the equal protection of the laws is a pledge of the protection of equal laws."

Although many of the Framers of the Fourteenth Amendment conceived of its primary function as bridging the vast distance between members of the Negro race and the white "majority," the Amendment itself was framed in universal terms, without reference to color, ethnic origin, or condition of prior servitude. As this Court recently remarked in interpreting the 1866 Civil Rights Act to extend to claims of racial discrimination against white persons, "the 39th Congress was intent upon establishing in the federal law a broader principle than would have been necessary simply to meet the particular and immediate plight of the newly freed Negro slaves." And that legislation was specifically broadened in 1870 to ensure that "all persons," not merely "citizens," would enjoy equal rights under the law. Indeed, it is not unlikely that among the Framers were many who would have applauded a reading of the Equal Protection Clause that states a principle of universal application and is responsive to the racial, ethnic, and cultural diversity of the Nation.

Over the past 30 years, this Court has embarked upon the crucial mission of interpreting the Equal Protection Clause with the view of assuring to all persons "the protection of equal laws" in a Nation confronting a legacy of slavery and racial discrimination. Because the landmark decisions in this area arose in response to the continued exclusion of Negroes from the mainstream of American society, they could be characterized as involving discrimination by the "majority" white race against the Negro minority. But they need not be read as depending upon that characterization for their results. It suffices to say that "[o]ver the years, this Court has consistently repudiated '[d]istinctions between citizens solely because of their ancestry' as being 'odious to a free people whose institutions are founded upon the doctrine of equality.'"

[The University] urges us to adopt for the first time a more restrictive view of the Equal Protection Clause and hold that discrimination against members of the white "majority" cannot be suspect if its purpose can be characterized as "benign." The clock of our liberties, however, cannot be turned back to 1868. It is far too late to argue

that the guarantee of equal protection to *all* persons permits the recognition of special wards entitled to a degree
of protection greater than that accorded others. "The
Fourteenth Amendment is not directed solely against discrimination due to a 'two-class theory' - that is, based
upon differences between 'white' and Negro."

Once the artificial line of a "two-class theory" of the
Fourteenth Amendment is put aside, the difficulties en-
tailed in varying the level of judicial review according to
a perceived "preferred" status of a particular racial or ethnic minority are intractable. The concepts of "majority"
and "minority" necessarily reflect temporary arrangements and political judgments. As observed above, the
white "majority" itself is composed of various minority
groups, most of which can lay claim to a history of prior
discrimination at the hands of the State and private individuals. Not all of these groups can receive preferential
treatment and corresponding judicial tolerance of distinctions drawn in terms of race and nationality, for then the
only "majority" left would be a new minority of white
Anglo-Saxon Protestants. There is no principled basis for
deciding which groups would merit "heightened judicial
solicitude" and which would not. Courts would be asked
to evaluate the extent of the prejudice and consequent
harm suffered by various minority groups. Those whose
societal injury is thought to exceed some arbitrary level of
tolerability then would be entitled to preferential classifications at the expense of individuals belonging to other
groups. Those classifications would be free from exacting
judicial scrutiny. As these preferences began to have
their desired effect, and the consequences of past discrimination were undone, new judicial rankings would be necessary. The kind of variable sociological and political
analysis necessary to produce such rankings simply does

not lie within the judicial competence - even if they otherwise were politically feasible and socially desirable.

Moreover, there are serious problems of justice connected with the idea of preference itself. First, it may not always be clear that a so-called preference is in fact benign. Courts may be asked to validate burdens imposed upon individual members of a particular group in order to advance the group's general interest. Nothing in the Constitution supports the notion that individuals may be asked to suffer otherwise impermissible burdens in order to enhance the societal standing of their ethnic groups. Second, preferential programs may only reinforce common stereotypes holding that certain groups are unable to achieve success without special protection based on a factor having no relationship to individual worth. Third, there is a measure of inequity in forcing innocent persons in [Bakke]'s position to bear the burdens of redressing grievances not of their making.

By hitching the meaning of the Equal Protection Clause to these transitory considerations, we would be holding, as a constitutional principle, that judicial scrutiny of classifications touching on racial and ethnic background may vary with the ebb and flow of political forces. Disparate constitutional tolerance of such classifications well may serve to exacerbate racial and ethnic antagonisms rather than alleviate them. Also, the mutability of a constitutional principle, based upon shifting political and social judgments, undermines the chances for consistent application of the Constitution from one generation to the next, a critical feature of its coherent interpretation. In expounding the Constitution, the Court's role is to discern "principles sufficiently absolute to give them roots throughout the community and continuity over significant periods of time, and to lift them above the level of the pragmatic political judgments of a particular time and place."

If it is the individual who is entitled to judicial protection against classifications based upon his racial or ethnic background because such distinctions impinge upon personal rights, rather than the individual only because of his membership in a particular group, then constitutional standards may be applied consistently. Political judgments regarding the necessity for the particular classification may be weighed in the constitutional balance, but the standard of justification will remain constant. This is as it should be, since those political judgments are the product of rough compromise struck by contending groups within the democratic process. When they touch upon an individual's race or ethnic background, he is entitled to a judicial determination that the burden he is asked to bear on that basis is precisely tailored to serve a compelling governmental interest. The Constitution guarantees that right to every person regardless of his background.

[The University] contends that on several occasions this Court has approved preferential classifications without applying the most exacting scrutiny. Most of the cases upon which petitioner relies are drawn from three areas: school desegregation, employment discrimination, and sex discrimination. Each of the cases cited presented a situation materially different from the facts of this case.

The school desegregation cases are inapposite. . . . The employment discrimination cases also do not advance petitioner's cause. . . . Nor is petitioner's view as to the applicable standard supported by the fact that gender-based classifications are not subjected to this level of scrutiny. . .

We have held that in "order to justify the use of a suspect classification, a State must show that its purpose or interest is both constitutionally permissible and substantial, and that its use of the classification is 'necessary ... to the accomplishment' of its purpose or the safeguarding of its interest."   The special admissions program purports to serve the purposes of: (i) "reducing the historic deficit of traditionally disfavored minorities in medical schools and in the medical profession"; (ii) countering the effects of societal discrimination; (iii) increasing the number of physicians who will practice in communities currently underserved; and (iv) obtaining the educational benefits that flow from an ethnically diverse student body. It is necessary to decide which, if any, of these purposes is substantial enough to support the use of a suspect classification.

If [the University]'s purpose is to assure within its student body some specified percentage of a particular group merely because of its race or ethnic origin, such a preferential purpose must be rejected not as unsubstantial but as facially invalid. Preferring members of any one group for no reason other than race or ethnic origin is discrimination for its own sake. This the Constitution forbids.

The State certainly has a legitimate and substantial interest in ameliorating, or eliminating where feasible, the disabling effects of identified discrimination. The line of school desegregation cases, commencing with *Brown*, attests to the importance of this state goal and the commitment of the judiciary to affirm all lawful means toward its attainment. In the school cases, the States were required by court order to redress the wrongs worked by specific instances of racial discrimination. That goal was far more focused than the remedying of the effects of "societal discrimination," an amorphous concept of injury that may be ageless in its reach into the past.

We have never approved a classification that aids persons perceived as members of relatively victimized groups at the expense of other innocent individuals in the absence of judicial, legislative, or administrative findings of constitutional or statutory violations. After such findings have been made, the governmental interest in preferring members of the injured groups at the expense of others is substantial, since the legal rights of the victims must be vindicated. In such a case, the extent of the injury and the consequent remedy will have been judicially, legislatively, or administratively defined. Also, the remedial action usually remains subject to continuing oversight to assure that it will work the least harm possible to other innocent persons competing for the benefit. Without such findings of constitutional or statutory violations, it cannot be said that the government has any greater interest in helping one individual than in refraining from harming another. Thus, the government has no compelling justification for inflicting such harm.

[The University] does not purport to have made, and is in no position to make, such findings. Its broad mission is education, not the formulation of any legislative policy or the adjudication of particular claims of illegality. For reasons similar to those stated [earlier in] this opinion, isolated segments of our vast governmental structures are not competent to make those decisions, at least in the absence of legislative mandates and legislatively determined criteria. Before relying upon these sorts of findings in establishing a racial classification, a governmental body must have the authority and capability to establish, in the record, that the classification is responsive to identified discrimination. Lacking this capability, [the University] has not carried its burden of justification on this issue.

Hence, the purpose of helping certain groups whom the faculty of the Davis Medical School perceived as victims of "societal discrimination" does not justify a classification that imposes disadvantages upon persons like [Bakke], who bear no responsibility for whatever harm the beneficiaries of the special admissions program are thought to have suffered. To hold otherwise would be to convert a remedy heretofore reserved for violations of legal rights into a privilege that all institutions throughout the Nation could grant at their pleasure to whatever groups are perceived as victims of societal discrimination. That is a step we have never approved.

[The University] identifies, as another purpose of its program, improving the delivery of health-care services to communities currently underserved. It may be assumed that in some situations a State's interest in facilitating the health care of its citizens is sufficiently compelling to support the use of a suspect classification. But there is virtually no evidence in the record indicating that petitioner's special admissions program is either needed or geared to promote that goal. The court below addressed this failure of proof:

> "The University concedes it cannot assure that minority doctors who entered under the program, all of whom expressed an 'interest' in practicing in a disadvantaged community, will actually do so. It may be correct to assume that some of them will carry out this intention, and that it is more likely they will practice in minority com-

munities than the average white doctor.
Nevertheless, there are more precise and
reliable ways to identify applicants who are
genuinely interested in the medical problems of minorities than by race. An applicant of whatever race who has demonstrated his concern for disadvantaged minorities
in the past and who declares that practice in
such a community is his primary professional goal would be more likely to contribute to alleviation of the medical shortage
than one who is chosen entirely on the basis
of race and disadvantage. In short, there is
no empirical data to demonstrate that any
one race is more selflessly socially oriented
or by contrast that another is more selfishly
acquisitive."

[The University] simply has not carried its burden of
demonstrating that it must prefer members of particular
ethnic groups over all other individuals in order to promote better health-care delivery to deprived citizens. Indeed, [the University] has not shown that its preferential
classification is likely to have any significant effect on
the problem.

The fourth goal asserted by petitioner is the attainment of
a diverse student body. This clearly is a constitutionally
permissible goal for an institution of higher education.
Academic freedom, though not a specifically enumerated
constitutional right, long has been viewed as a special concern of the First Amendment. The freedom of a university to make its own judgments as to education includes the
selection of its student body. Justice Frankfurter summa-

rized the "four essential freedoms" that constitute academic freedom:

> "'It is the business of a university to provide that atmosphere which is most conducive to speculation, experiment and creation. It is an atmosphere in which there prevail "the four essential freedoms" of a university - to determine for itself on academic grounds who may teach, what may be taught, how it shall be taught, and who may be admitted to study.'"

Our national commitment to the safeguarding of these freedoms within university communities was emphasized in *Keyishian v. Board of Regents* (1967):

> "Our Nation is deeply committed to safeguarding academic freedom which is of transcendent value to all of us and not merely to the teachers concerned. That freedom is therefore a special concern of the First Amendment. . . . The Nation's future depends upon leaders trained through wide exposure to that robust exchange of ideas which discovers truth 'out of a multitude of tongues, [rather] than through any kind of authoritative selection.'"

The atmosphere of "speculation, experiment and creation" - so essential to the quality of higher education - is widely believed to be promoted by a diverse student body. As the Court noted in *Keyishian*, it is not too much to say that the "nation's future depends upon leaders trained through wide exposure" to the ideas and mores of students as diverse as this Nation of many peoples.

Thus, in arguing that its universities must be accorded the right to select those students who will contribute the most to the "robust exchange of ideas," [the University] invokes a countervailing constitutional interest, that of the First Amendment. In this light, petitioner must be viewed as seeking to achieve a goal that is of paramount importance in the fulfillment of its mission.

It may be argued that there is greater force to these views at the undergraduate level than in a medical school where the training is centered primarily on professional competency. But even at the graduate level, our tradition and experience lend support to the view that the contribution of diversity is substantial. In *Sweatt v. Painter*, the Court made a similar point with specific reference to legal education:

> "The law school, the proving ground for legal learning and practice, cannot be effective in isolation from the individuals and institutions with which the law interacts. Few students and no one who has practiced law would choose to study in an academic vacuum, removed from the interplay of ideas and the exchange of views with which the law is concerned."

Physicians serve a heterogeneous population. An otherwise qualified medical student with a particular background - whether it be ethnic, geographic, culturally advantaged or disadvantaged - may bring to a professional school of medicine experiences, outlooks, and ideas that enrich the training of its student body and better equip its graduates to render with understanding their vital service to humanity.

Ethnic diversity, however, is only one element in a range of factors a university properly may consider in attaining the goal of a heterogeneous student body. Although a university must have wide discretion in making the sensitive judgments as to who should be admitted, constitutional limitations protecting individual rights may not be disregarded. [Bakke] urges - and the courts below have held - that [the University]'s dual admissions program is a racial classification that impermissibly infringes his rights under the Fourteenth Amendment. As the interest of diversity is compelling in the context of a university's admissions program, the question remains whether the program's racial classification is necessary to promote this interest.

It may be assumed that the reservation of a specified number of seats in each class for individuals from the preferred ethnic groups would contribute to the attainment of considerable ethnic diversity in the student body. But petitioner's argument that this is the only effective means of serving the interest of diversity is seriously flawed. In a most fundamental sense the argument misconceives the nature of the state interest that would justify consideration of race or ethnic background. It is not an interest in simple ethnic diversity, in which a specified percentage of the student body is in effect guaranteed to be members of selected ethnic groups, with the remaining percentage an undifferentiated aggregation of students. The diversity that furthers a compelling state interest encompasses a far broader array of qualifications and characteristics of which racial or ethnic origin is but a single though important element. Petitioner's special admissions program, focused *solely* on ethnic diversity, would hinder rather than further attainment of genuine diversity.

Nor would the state interest in genuine diversity be served by expanding [the University]'s two-track system into a multitrack program with a prescribed number of seats set aside for each identifiable category of applicants. Indeed, it is inconceivable that a university would thus pursue the logic of [the University]'s two-track program to the illogical end of insulating each category of applicants with certain desired qualifications from competition with all other applicants.

The experience of other university admissions programs, which take race into account in achieving the educational diversity valued by the First Amendment, demonstrates that the assignment of a fixed number of places to a minority group is not a necessary means toward that end. An illuminating example is found in the Harvard College program:

> "In recent years Harvard College has expanded the concept of diversity to include students from disadvantaged economic, racial and ethnic groups. Harvard College now recruits not only Californians or Louisianans but also blacks and Chicanos and other minority students. . . .

> "In practice, this new definition of diversity has meant that race has been a factor in some admission decisions. When the Committee on Admissions reviews the large middle group of applicants who are

'admissible' and deemed capable of doing good work in their courses, the race of an applicant may tip the balance in his favor just as geographic origin or a life spent on a farm may tip the balance in other candidates' cases. A farm boy from Idaho can bring something to Harvard College that a Bostonian cannot offer. Similarly, a black student can usually bring something that a white person cannot offer. . . .

"In Harvard College admissions the Committee has not set target-quotas for the number of blacks, or of musicians, football players, physicists or Californians to be admitted in a given year. . . . But that awareness [of the necessity of including more than a token number of black students] does not mean that the Committee sets a minimum number of blacks or of people from west of the Mississippi who are to be admitted. It means only that in choosing among thousands of applicants who are not only 'admissible' academically but have other strong qualities, the Committee, with a number of criteria in mind, pays some attention to distribution among many types and categories of students."

In such an admissions program, race or ethnic background may be deemed a "plus" in a particular applicant's file, yet it does not insulate the individual from comparison with all other candidates for the available seats. The file of a particular black applicant may be examined for his potential contribution to diversity without the factor of race being decisive when compared, for example, with that of an applicant identified as an Italian-American if the latter is thought to exhibit qualities more likely to promote beneficial educational pluralism. Such qualities could include exceptional personal talents, unique work or service experience, leadership potential, maturity, demonstrated compassion, a history of overcoming disadvantage, ability to communicate with the poor, or other qualifications deemed important. In short, an admissions program operated in this way is flexible enough to consider all pertinent elements of diversity in light of the particular qualifications of each applicant, and to place them on the same footing for consideration, although not necessarily according them the same weight. Indeed, the weight attributed to a particular quality may vary from year to year depending upon the "mix" both of the student body and the applicants for the incoming class.

This kind of program treats each applicant as an individual in the admissions process. The applicant who loses out on the last available a seat to another candidate receiving a "plus" on the basis of ethnic background will not have been foreclosed from all consideration for that seat simply because he was not the right color or had the wrong surname. It would mean only that his combined qualifications, which may have included similar nonobjective factors, did not outweigh those of the other applicant. His qualifications would have been weighed fairly and competitively, and he would have no basis to complain of unequal treatment under the Fourteenth Amendment.

It has been suggested that an admissions program which considers race only as one factor is simply a subtle and more sophisticated - but no less effective - means of according racial preference than the Davis program. A facial intent to discriminate, however, is evident in [the University]'s preference program and not denied in this case. No such facial infirmity exists in an admissions program where race or ethnic background is simply one element - to be weighed fairly against other elements - in the selection process. "A boundary line," as Justice Frankfurter remarked in another connection, "is none the worse for being narrow." And a court would not assume that a university, professing to employ a facially nondiscriminatory admissions policy, would operate it as a cover for the functional equivalent of a quota system. In short, good faith would be presumed in the absence of a showing to the contrary in the manner permitted by our cases.

In summary, it is evident that the Davis special admissions program involves the use of an explicit racial classification never before countenanced by this Court. It tells applicants who are not Negro, Asian, or Chicano that they are totally excluded from a specific percentage of the seats in an entering class. No matter how strong their qualifications, quantitative and extracurricular, including their own potential for contribution to educational diversity, they are never afforded the chance to compete with applicants from the preferred groups for the special admissions seats. At the same time, the preferred applicants have the opportunity to compete for every seat in the class.

The fatal flaw in [the University]'s preferential program is its disregard of individual rights as guaranteed by the Fourteenth Amendment. Such rights are not absolute. But when a State's distribution of benefits or imposition of burdens hinges on ancestry or the color of a person's skin, that individual is entitled to a demonstration that the challenged classification is necessary to promote a substantial state interest. [The University] has failed to carry this burden. For this reason, that portion of the California court's judgment holding petitioner's special admissions program invalid under the Fourteenth Amendment must be affirmed.

In enjoining [the University] from ever considering the race of any applicant, however, the courts below failed to recognize that the State has a substantial interest that legitimately may be served by a properly devised admissions program involving the competitive consideration of race and ethnic origin. For this reason, so much of the California court's judgment as enjoins petitioner from any consideration of the race of any applicant must be reversed.

With respect to [Bakke]'s entitlement to an injunction [order] directing his admission to the Medical School, [the University] has conceded that it could not carry its burden of proving that, but for the existence of its unlawful special admissions program, [Bakke] still would not have been admitted. Hence, [Bakke] is entitled to the injunction, and that portion of the judgment must be affirmed.

BOOK BANNING

BOARD OF EDUCATION v. PICO

The Book Banning Decision originates on Long Island, New York. The Board of Education of the Island Trees Union Free School District, ordered, against the recommendations of a committee of parents and school staff, the removal from the high school and junior high school libraries of nine books characterized as "anti-American, anti-Christian, anti-Semitic, and just plain filthy".

Students at the schools, including Steven Pico, sued the Board in U.S. District Court claiming a denial of their First Amendment rights. The District Court found in favor of the School Board. The students appealed to the U.S. Court of Appeals which reversed the decision. The School Board appealed to the U.S. Supreme Court which granted a review.

Oral arguments were heard March 2 and the decision was announced June 25, 1982.

Justice William Brennan announced the decision of the Court. Justices Thurgood Marshall, John Paul Stevens, and Byron White concurred. Justice Harry Blackmun concurred in part. Chief Justice Burger and Justices Lewis Powell, William Rehnquist, and Sandra Day O'Connor dissented.

The full text of *Board of Education v. Pico* can be found in United States Reports, volume 457, page 853.

BOARD OF EDUCATION v. PICO

June 25, 1982

JUSTICE WILLIAM BRENNAN: The principal question presented is whether the First Amendment imposes limitations upon the exercise by a local school board of its discretion to remove library books from high school and junior high school libraries.

Petitioners are the Board of Education of the Island Trees Union Free School District No. 26, in New York, and . . . [Richard Ahrens,] the President of the Board, . . . [Frank Martin,] the Vice President, and . . . [other] Board members. The Board is a state agency charged with responsibility for the operation and administration of the public schools within the Island Trees School District. . . . Respondents are Steven Pico, Jacqueline Gold, Glenn Yarris, Russell Rieger, and Paul Sochinski . . . , students at the High School, and . . . Junior High School.

In September 1975, petitioners Ahrens, Martin, and [other School Board members] attended a conference sponsored by Parents of New York United (PONYU), a politically conservative organization of parents concerned about education legislation in the State of New York. At the conference these petitioners obtained lists of books described by Ahrens as "objectionable," and by Martin as "improper fare for school students." It was later determined that the High School library contained nine of the listed books [Slaughter House Five, The Naked Ape, Down These Mean Streets, Best Short Stories of Negro Writers, Go Ask Alice, Laughing Boy, Black Boy, A Hero Ain't Nothin' But a Sandwich, and Soul on Ice], and that another listed book [A Reader for Writers] was in the Junior High

School library. In February 1976, at a meeting with the
Superintendent of Schools and the Principals of the High
School and Junior High School, the Board gave an
"unofficial direction" that the listed books be removed
from the library shelves and delivered to the Board's offices, so that Board members could read them. When this
directive was carried out, it became publicized, and the
Board issued a press release justifying its action. It characterized the removed books as "anti-American, anti-
Christian, anti-Semitic, and just plain filthy," and concluded that "[i]t is our duty, our moral obligation, to protect
the children in our schools from this moral danger as
surely as from physical and medical dangers."

A short time later, the Board appointed a "Book Review
Committee," consisting of four Island Trees parents and
four members of the Island Trees schools staff, to read
the listed books and to recommend to the Board whether
the books should be retained, taking into account the
books' "educational suitability," "good taste," "relevance,"
and "appropriateness to age and grade level." In July, the
Committee made its final report to the Board, recommending that five of the listed books be retained and that
two others be removed from the school libraries. As for
the remaining four books, the Committee could not agree
on two, took no position on one, and recommended that
the last book be made available to students only with parental approval.   The Board substantially rejected the
Committee's report later that month, deciding that only
one book should be returned to the High School library
without restriction, that another should be made available
subject to parental approval, but that the remaining nine
books should "be removed from elementary and secondary
libraries and [from] use in the curriculum." The Board

gave no reasons for rejecting the recommendations of the Committee that it had appointed.

Respondents reacted to the Board's decision by bringing the present action. They alleged that petitioners had

> "ordered the removal of the books from school libraries and proscribed [prohibited] their use in the curriculum because particular passages in the books offended their social, political and moral tastes and not because the books, taken as a whole, were lacking in educational value."

[Pico and his fellow students] claimed that the Board's actions denied them their rights under the First Amendment. They asked the court for a declaration that the Board's actions were unconstitutional, and for [the court to order] the Board to return the nine books to the school libraries and to refrain from interfering with the use of those books in the schools' curricula.

The District Court granted summary [immediate] judgment in favor of [the School Board]. In the court's view, "the parties substantially agree[d] about the motivation behind the board's actions," - namely, that

> "the board acted not on religious principles but on its conservative educational philosophy, and on its belief that the nine books removed from the school library and curriculum were irrelevant, vulgar, immoral, and in bad taste, making them educationally unsuitable for the district's junior and senior high school students."

With this factual premise as its background, the court rejected [the students'] contention that their First Amendment rights had been infringed by the Board's actions. Noting that statutes, history, and precedent had vested local school boards with a broad discretion to formulate educational policy, the court concluded that it should not intervene in "'the daily operations of school systems'" unless "'basic constitutional values'" were "'sharply implicate[d]'," and determined that the conditions for such intervention did not exist in the present case. Acknowledging that the "removal [of the books] . . . clearly was content-based," the court nevertheless found no constitutional violation of the requisite magnitude:

> "The board has restricted access only to certain books which the board believed to be, in essence, vulgar. While removal of such books from a school library may . . . reflect a misguided educational philosophy, it does not constitute a sharp and direct infringement of any first amendment right."

A three-judge panel of the United States Court of Appeals . . . reversed the judgment of the District Court. . . . Judge Newman . . . viewed the case as turning on the contested factual issue of whether petitioners' removal decision was motivated by a justifiable desire to remove books containing vulgarities and sexual explicitness, or rather by an impermissible desire to suppress ideas.

. . . . Our precedents have long recognized certain constitutional limits upon the power of the State to control even the curriculum and classroom. For example, *Meyer v. Nebraska* (1923) struck down a state law that forbade the teaching of modern foreign languages in public and private schools, and *Epperson v. Arkansas* (1968) declared unconstitutional a state law that prohibited the teaching of the Darwinian theory of evolution in any state-supported school. But the current action does not require us to re-enter this difficult terrain, which *Meyer* and *Epperson* traversed without apparent misgiving. For as this case is presented to us, it does not involve textbooks, or indeed any books that Island Trees students would be required to read. [The students] do not seek in this Court to impose limitations upon their school Board's discretion to prescribe the curricula of the Island Trees schools. On the contrary, the only books at issue in this case are *library* books, books that by their nature are optional rather than required reading. Our adjudication of the present case thus does not intrude into the classroom, or into the compulsory courses taught there. Furthermore, even as to library books, the action before us does not involve the *acquisition* of books. Respondents have not sought to compel their school Board to add to the school library shelves any books that students desire to read. Rather, the only action challenged in this case is the *removal* from school libraries of books originally placed there by the school authorities, or without objection from them.

.... [T]he issue before us ... is a narrow one. ... [D]oes the First Amendment impose *any* limitations upon the discretion of [the School Board] to remove library books from the Island Trees High School and Junior High School? ...

The Court has long recognized that local school boards have broad discretion in the management of school affairs. *Epperson* ... reaffirmed that, by and large, "public education in our Nation is committed to the control of state and local authorities," and that federal courts should not ordinarily "intervene in the resolution of conflicts which arise in the daily operation of school systems." *Tinker v. Des Moines School District* noted that we have "repeatedly emphasized . . . the comprehensive authority of the States and of school officials . . . to prescribe and control conduct in the schools." We have also acknowledged that public schools are vitally important "in the preparation of individuals for participation as citizens," and as vehicles for "inculcating fundamental values necessary to the maintenance of a democratic political system." We are therefore in full agreement with petitioners that local school boards must be permitted "to establish and apply their curriculum in such a way as to transmit community values," and that "there is a legitimate and substantial community interest in promoting respect for authority and traditional values be they social, moral, or political."

At the same time, however, we have necessarily recognized that the discretion of the States and local school boards in matters of education must be exercised in a manner that comports with the transcendent imperatives of the First Amendment. In *West Virginia Board of Education v. Barnette* (1943), we held that under the First Amendment a student in a public school could not be compelled to salute the flag. We reasoned:

> "Boards of Education . . . have, of course, important, delicate, and highly discretionary functions, but none that they may not perform within the limits of the Bill of Rights. That they are educating the young for citizenship is reason for scrupulous protection of Constitutional freedoms of the individual, if we are not to strangle the free mind at its source and teach youth to discount im-

portant principles of our government as
mere platitudes."

Later cases have consistently followed this rationale.
Thus *Epperson* . . . invalidated a State's anti-evolution
statute as violative of the Establishment Clause, and reaffirmed the duty of federal courts "to apply the First
Amendment's mandate in our educational system where
essential to safeguard the fundamental values of freedom
of speech and inquiry." And *Tinker* . . . held that a local
school board had infringed the free speech rights of high
school and junior high school students by suspending
them from school for wearing black armbands in class as
a protest against the Government's policy in Vietnam; we
stated there that the "comprehensive authority . . . of
school officials" must be exercised "consistent with fundamental constitutional safeguards." In sum, students do not
"shed their constitutional rights to freedom of speech or
expression at the schoolhouse gate," and therefore local
school boards must discharge their "important, delicate,
and highly discretionary functions" within the limits and
constraints of the First Amendment.

The nature of students' First Amendment rights in the
context of this case requires further examination. . . .
Barnette is instructive. There the Court held that students' liberty of conscience could not be infringed in the
name of "national unity" or "patriotism." We explained
that

> "the action of the local authorities in com-
> pelling the flag salute and pledge transcends
> constitutional limitations on their power
> and invades the sphere of intellect and spir-
> it which it is the purpose of the First

Amendment to our Constitution to reserve
from all official control."

Similarly, *Tinker*... held that students' rights to freedom
of expression of their political views could not be
abridged by reliance upon an "undifferentiated fear or ap-
prehension of disturbance" arising from such expression:

> "Any departure from absolute regimenta-
> tion may cause trouble. Any variation from
> the majority's opinion may inspire fear.
> Any word spoken, in class, in the lunch-
> room, or on the campus, that deviates from
> the views of another person may start an ar-
> gument or cause a disturbance. But our
> Constitution says we must take this risk;
> and our history says that it is this sort of
> hazardous freedom - this kind of openness -
> that is the basis of our national strength and
> of the independence and vigor of Ameri-
> cans who grow up and live in this . . . often
> disputatious society."

In short, "First Amendment rights, applied in light of the
special characteristics of the school environment, are
available to . . . students."

Of course, courts should not "intervene in the resolution
of conflicts which arise in the daily operation of school
systems" unless "basic constitutional values" are "directly
and sharply implicate[d]" in those conflicts. But we think
that the First Amendment rights of students may be directly and sharply implicated by the removal of books
from the shelves of a school library. Our precedents have
focused "not only on the role of the First Amendment in

fostering individual self-expression but also on its role in affording the public access to discussion, debate, and the dissemination of information and ideas." And we have recognized that "the State may not, consistently with the spirit of the First Amendment, contract the spectrum of available knowledge." In keeping with this principle, we have held that in a variety of contexts "the Constitution protects the right to receive information and ideas." This right is an inherent corollary of the rights of free speech and press that are explicitly guaranteed by the Constitution, in two senses. First, the right to receive ideas follows ineluctably from the *sender's* First Amendment right to send them: "The right of freedom of speech and press . . . embraces the right to distribute literature, and necessarily protects the right to receive it." "The dissemination of ideas can accomplish nothing if otherwise willing addressees are not free to receive and consider them. It would be a barren marketplace of ideas that had only sellers and no buyers."

More importantly, the right to receive ideas is a necessary predicate to the *recipient's* meaningful exercise of his own rights of speech, press, and political freedom. Madison admonished us:

> "A popular Government, without popular information, or the means of acquiring it, is but a Prologue to a Farce or a Tragedy; or, perhaps both. Knowledge will forever govern ignorance: And a people who mean to be their own Governors, must arm themselves with the power which knowledge gives."

As we recognized in *Tinker*, students too are beneficiaries of this principle:

> "In our system, students may not be regarded as closed-circuit recipients of only that which the State chooses to communicate. . . . [S]chool officials cannot suppress 'expressions of feeling with which they do not wish to contend.'"

In sum, just as access to ideas makes it possible for citizens generally to exercise their rights of free speech and press in a meaningful manner, such access prepares students for active and effective participation in the pluralistic, often contentious society in which they will soon be adult members. Of course all First Amendment rights accorded to students must be construed "in light of the special characteristics of the school environment." But the special characteristics of the school *library* make that environment especially appropriate for the recognition of the First Amendment rights of students.

A school library, no less than any other public library, is "a place dedicated to quiet, to knowledge, and to beauty." *Keyishian v. Board of Regents* (1967) observed that "'students must always remain free to inquire, to study and to evaluate, to gain new maturity and understanding.'" The school library is the principal locus of such freedom. As one District Court has well put it, in the school library

> "a student can literally explore the unknown, and discover areas of interest and thought not covered by the prescribed curriculum. . . . Th[e] student learns that a library is a place to test or expand upon ideas

presented to him, in or out of the classroom."

[The School Board] emphasize[s] the inculcative function
of secondary education, and argue[s] that [it] must be allowed *unfettered* discretion to "transmit community
values" through the Island Trees schools. But that sweeping claim overlooks the unique role of the school library.
It appears from the record that use of the Island Trees
school libraries is completely voluntary on the part of students. Their selection of books from these libraries is entirely a matter of free choice; the libraries afford them an
opportunity at self-education and individual enrichment
that is wholly optional. Petitioners might well defend
their claim of absolute discretion in matters of *curriculum*
by reliance upon their duty to inculcate community
values. But we think that petitioners' reliance upon that
duty is misplaced where, as here, they attempt to extend
their claim of absolute discretion beyond the compulsory
environment of the classroom, into the school library and
the regime of voluntary inquiry that there holds sway.

In rejecting [the School Board's] claim of absolute discretion to remove books from their school libraries, we do
not deny that local school boards have a substantial legitimate role to play in the determination of school library
content. We thus must turn to the question of the extent
to which the First Amendment places limitations upon the
discretion of [the School Board] to remove books from
their libraries. In this inquiry we enjoy the guidance of
several precedents. . . . *Barnette* stated:

"If there is any fixed star in our constitutional constellation, it is that no official,
high or petty, can prescribe what shall be

orthodox in politics, nationalism, religion, or
other matters of opinion. . . . If there are
any circumstances which permit an exception, they do not now occur to us."

This doctrine has been reaffirmed in later cases involving
education. For example, *Keyishian* . . . noted that "the
First Amendment . . . does not tolerate laws that cast a
pall of orthodoxy over the classroom." And *Mt. Healthy
City Board of Education v. Doyle* (1977) recognized First
Amendment limitations upon the discretion of a local
school board to refuse to rehire a nontenured teacher.
The school board in *Mt. Healthy* had declined to renew respondent Doyle's employment contract, in part because he
had exercised his First Amendment rights. Although
Doyle did not have tenure, and thus "could have been discharged for no reason whatever," *Mt. Healthy* held that he
could "nonetheless establish a claim to reinstatement if
the decision not to rehire him was made by reason of his
exercise of constitutionally protected First Amendment
freedoms." We held further that once Doyle had shown
"that his conduct was constitutionally protected, and that
this conduct was a 'substantial factor' . . . in the Board's
decision not to rehire him," the school board was obliged
to show "by a preponderance of the evidence that it would
have reached the same decision as to respondent's reem-
ployment even in the absence of the protected conduct."

With respect to the present case, the message of these
precedents is clear. [The School Board] rightly possess[es]
significant discretion to determine the content of their
school libraries. But that discretion may not be exercised
in a narrowly partisan or political manner. If a Democratic school board, motivated by party affiliation, ordered
the removal of all books written by or in favor of Repub-

licans, few would doubt that the order violated the constitutional rights of the students denied access to those books. The same conclusion would surely apply if an all-white school board, motivated by racial animus, decided to remove all books authored by blacks or advocating racial equality and integration. Our Constitution does not permit the official suppression of *ideas*. Thus whether [the School Board's] removal of books from their school libraries denied [the students] their First Amendment rights depends upon the motivation behind [the School Board's] actions. If [the School Board] *intended* by [its] removal decision to deny [the students] access to ideas with which [the School Board] disagreed, and if this intent was the decisive factor in [the School Board's] decision, then [the School Board has] exercised [its] discretion in violation of the Constitution. To permit such intentions to control official actions would be to encourage the precise sort of officially prescribed orthodoxy unequivocally condemned in *Barnette*. On the other hand, [the students] implicitly concede that an unconstitutional motivation would *not* be demonstrated if it were shown that [the School Board] had decided to remove the books at issue because those books were pervasively vulgar. And again, [the students] concede that if it were demonstrated that the removal decision was based solely upon the "educational suitability" of the books in question, then their removal would be "perfectly permissible." In other words, in [the students'] view such motivations, if decisive of [the School Board's] actions, would not carry the danger of an official suppression of ideas, and thus would not violate [the students'] First Amendment rights.

As noted earlier, nothing in our decision today affects in any way the discretion of a local school board to choose books to *add* to the libraries of their schools. Because we are concerned in this case with the suppression of ideas, our holding today affects only the discretion to *remove* books. In brief, we hold that local school boards may not remove books from school library shelves simply because they dislike the ideas contained in those books and seek by their removal to "prescribe what shall be orthodox in politics, nationalism, religion, or other matters of opinion." Such purposes stand inescapably condemned by our precedents. . . . *Affirmed.*

FLAG BURNING

TEXAS v. JOHNSON

The Flag Burning Decision originates in Texas. During the 1984 Republican National Convention in Dallas Gregory Lee Johnson publicly burned the American Flag as a means of political protest.

Johnson was charged with the crime, under Texas law, of desecration of a venerated object. He was tried, found guilty, fined and sentenced to prison. The Texas Court of Criminal Appeals reversed the conviction as a violation of Johnson's First Amendment rights. The State of Texas appealed to the U.S. Supreme Court which granted a review.

Oral arguments were heard March 21, 1989 and a decision was announced June 21.

Justice Brennan delivered the opinion of the Court. Justices Thurgood Marshall, Harry Blackmun, Antonin Scalia, and Anthony Kennedy concurred. Justices William Rehnquist, Sandra Day O'Connor, and John Paul Stevens dissented.

TEXAS v. JOHNSON

June 21, 1989

JUSTICE WILLIAM BRENNAN: After publicly burning an American flag as a means of political protest, Gregory Lee Johnson was convicted of desecrating a flag in violation of Texas law. This case presents the question whether his conviction is consistent with the First Amendment. We hold that it is not.

While the Republican Convention was taking place in Dallas in 1984, respondent Johnson participated in a political demonstration dubbed the "Republican War Chest Tour." As explained in literature distributed by the demonstrators and in speeches made by them, the purpose of this event was to protest the policies of the Reagan administration and of certain Dallas-based corporations. The demonstratores marched through the Dallas streets, chanting political slogans and stopping at several corporate locations to stage "die-ins" intended to dramatize the consequences of nuclear war. On several occasions they spray-painted the walls of buildings and overturned potted plants, but Johnson himself took no part in such activities. He did, however, accept an American flag handed to him by a fellow protestor who had taken it from a flag pole outside one of the targeted buildings.

The demonstration ended in front of Dallas City Hall, where Johnson unfurled the American flag, doused it with kerosene, and set it on fire. While the flag burned, the protestors chanted, "America, the red, white, and blue, we spit on you." After the demonstrators dispersed, a witness to the flag-burning collected the flag's remains and buried them in his back yard. No one was physically injured or threatened with injury, though several witnesses testified that they had been seriously offended by the flag-burning.

Of the approximately 100 demonstrators, Johnson alone was charged with a crime. The only criminal offense with which he was charged was the desecration of a venerated object in violation of Texas Penal Code Ann. [Section] 42.09(a)(3)(1989). After a trial, he was convicted, sentenced to one year in prison, and fined $2,000. The Court of Appeals for the Fifth District of Texas at Dallas affirmed [let stand] Johnson's conviction, but the Texas Court of Criminal Appeals reversed, holding that the State could not, consistent with the First Amendment, punish Johnson for burning the flag in these circumstances.

The Court of Criminal Appeals began by recognizing that Johnson's conduct was symbolic speech protected by the First Amendment: "Given the context of an organized demonstration, speeches, slogans, and the distribution of literature, anyone who observed [Johnson]'s act would have understood the message that [Johnson] intended to convey. The act for which [Johnson] was convicted was clearly 'speech' contemplated by the First Amendment. To justify Johnson's conviction for engaging in symbolic speech, the State asserted two interests: preserving the flag as a symbol of national unity and preventing breaches of the peace. The Court of Criminal Appeals held that neither interest supported his conviction.

Acknowledging that this Court had not yet decided whether the Government may criminally sanction flag desecration in order to preserve the flag's symbolic value, the Texas court nevertheless concluded that our decision in *West Virginia Board of Education v. Barnette* (1943) suggested that furthering this interest by curtailing speech was impermissible. "Recognizing that the right to differ is the centerpiece of our First Amendment freedoms," the court explained, "a government cannot mandate by fiat a feeling of unity in its citizens. Therefore, that very same government cannot carve out a symbol of unity and prescribe a set of approved messages to be associated with that symbol when it cannot mandate the status or feeling the symbol purports to represent." Noting that the State had not shown that the flag was in "grave and immediate danger" of being stripped of its symbolic value, the Texas court also decided that the flag's special status was not endangered by Johnson's conduct.

As to the State's goal of preventing breaches of the peace, the court concluded that the flag-desecration statute was not drawn narrowly enough to encompass only those flag-burnings that were likely to result in a serious disturbance of the peace. And in fact, the court emphasized, the flag burning in this particular case did not threaten such a reaction. "'Serious offense' occurred," the court admitted, "but there was no breach of peace nor does the record reflect that the situation was potentially explosive. One cannot equate 'serious offense' with incitement to breach the peace. . . .

Johnson was convicted of flag desecration for burning the flag rather than for uttering insulting words. This fact somewhat complicates our consideration of his conviction under the First Amendment. We must first determine whether Johnson's burning of the flag constituted expressive conduct, permitting him to invoke the First Amendment in challenging his conviction. If his conduct was expressive, we next decide whether the State's regulation is related to the suppression of free expression. If the State's regulation is not related to expression, then the less stringent standard we announced in *United States v. O'Brien* for regulations of noncommunicative conduct controls. If it is, then we are outside of *O'Brien's* test, and we must ask whether this interest justifies Johnson's conviction under a more demanding standard. A third possibility is that the State's asserted interest is simply not implicated on these facts, and in that event the interest drops out of the picture.

The First Amendment literally forbids the abridgement only of "speech," but we have long recognized that its protection does not end at the spoken or written word. While we have rejected "the view that an apparently limitless variety of conduct can be labeled 'speech' whenever the person engaging in the conduct intends thereby to express an idea," we have acknowledged that conduct may be "sufficiently imbued with elements of communication to fall within the scope of the First and Fourteenth Amendments."

In deciding whether particular conduct possesses sufficient communicative elements to bring the First Amendment into play, we have asked whether "[a]n intent to convey a particularized message was present, and [whether] the likelihood was great that the message would be understood by those who viewed it." Hence, we have recognized the expressive nature of students' wearing of black armbands to protest American military involvement in Vietnam; of a sit-in by blacks in a "whites only" area to protest segregation; of the wearing of American military uniforms in a dramatic presentation criticizing American involvement in Vietnam; and of picketing about a wide variety of causes.

Especially pertinent to this case are our decisions recognizing the communicative nature of conduct relating to flags. Attaching a peace sign to the flag; saluting the flag; and displaying a red flag, we have held, all may find shelter under the First Amendment. That we have had little difficulty identifying an expressive element in conduct relating to flags should not be surprising. The very purpose of a national flag is to serve as a symbol of our country; it is, one might say, "the one visible manifestation of two hundred years of nationhood." Thus, we have observed:

> "[T]he flag is a form of utterance. Symbolism is a primitive but effective way of communicating idea. The use of an emblem or flag to symbolize some system, idea, institution, or personality, is a short cut from mind to mind. Causes and nations, political parties, lodges and ecclesiastical groups seek to knit the loyalty of their followings to a flag or banner, a color or design."

Pregnant with expressive content, the flag as readily signifies this Nation as does the combination of letters found in "America."

We have not automatically concluded, however, that any action taken with respect to our flag is expressive. Instead, in characterizing such action for First Amendment purposes, we have considered the context in which it occurred. In *Spence,* for example, we emphasized that Spence's taping of a peace sign to his flag was "roughly simultaneous with and concededly triggered by the Cambodian incursion and the Kent State tragedy." The State of Washington had conceded, in fact, that Spence's conduct was a form of communication, and we stated that "the State's concession is inevitable on this record."

The State of Texas conceded for purposes of its oral argument in this case that Johnson's conduct was expressive conduct, and this concession seems to us as prudent as was Washington's in *Spence*. Johnson burned an American flag as part - indeed, as the culmination - of a political demonstration that coincided with the convening of the Republican Party and its renomination of Ronald Reagan for President. The expressive, overtly political nature of this conduct was both intentional and overwhelmingly apparent. At his trial, Johnson explained his reasons for burning the flag as follows: "The American Flag was burned as Ronald Reagan was being renominated as President. And a more powerful statement of symbolic speech, whether you agree with it or not, couldn't have been made at that time. It's quite a just position [juxtaposition]. We had new patriotism and no patriotism." In these circumstances, Johnson's burning of the flag was conduct "sufficiently imbued with elements of communication" to implicate the First Amendment.

The Government generally has a freer hand in restricting expressive conduct than it has in restricting the written or spoken word. It may not, however, proscribe [prohibit] particular conduct *because* it has expressive elements. "[W]hat might be termed the more generalized guarantee of freedom of expression makes the communicative nature of conduct an inadequate *basis* for singling out that conduct for proscription. A law *directed at* the communicative nature of conduct must, like a law directed at speech itself, be justified by the substantial showing of need that the First Amendment requires." It is, in short, not simply the verbal or nonverbal nature of the expression, but the governmental interest at stake, that helps to determine whether a restriction on that expression is valid.

Thus, although we have recognized that where "'speech' and 'nonspeech' elements are combined in the same course of conduct, a sufficiently important governmental interest in regulating the nonspeech element can justify incidental limitations on First Amendment freedoms," we have limited the applicability of *O'Brien*'s relatively lenient standard to those cases in which "the governmental interest is unrelated to the suppression of free expression." In stating, moreover, that *O'Brien*'s test "in the last analysis is little, if any, different from the standard applied to time, place, or manner restrictions," we have highlighted the requirement that the governmental interest in question be unconnected to expression in order to come under *O'Brien*'s less demanding rule.

In order to decide whether *O'Brien*'s test applies here, therefore, we must decide whether Texas has asserted an interest in support of Johnson's conviction that is unrelated to the suppression of expression. If we find that an interest asserted by the State is simply not implicated on the facts before us, we need not ask whether *O'Brien*'s test applies. The State offers two separate interests to justify this conviction: preventing breaches of the peace, and preserving the flag as a symbol of nationhood and national unity. We hold that the first interest is not implicated on this record and that the second is related to the suppression of expression.

Texas claims that its interest in preventing breaches of the peace justifies Johnson's conviction for flag desecration. However, no disturbance of the peace actually occurred or threatened to occur because of Johnson's burning of the flag. Although the State stresses the disruptive behavior of the protestors during their march toward City Hall, it admits that "no actual breach of the peace occurred at the time of the flagburning or in response to the flagburning." The State's emphasis on the protestors' disorderly actions prior to arriving at City Hall is not only somewhat surprising given that no charges were brought on the basis of this conduct, but it also fails to show that a disturbance of the peace was a likely reaction to *Johnson's* conduct. The only evidence offered by the State at trial to show the reaction to Johnson's actions was the testimony of several persons who had been seriously offended by the flag-burning.

The State's position, therefore, amounts to a claim that an audience that takes serious offense at particular expression is necessarily likely to disturb the peace and that the expression may be prohibited on this basis. Our precedents do not countenance such a presumption. On the contrary, they recognize that a principal "function of free speech under our system of government is to invite dispute. It may indeed best serve its high purpose when it induces a condition of unrest, creates dissatisfaction with conditions as they are, or even stirs people to anger." It would be odd indeed to conclude *both* that "if it is the speaker's opinion that gives offense, that consequence is a reason for according it constitutional protection," *and* that the Government may ban the expression of certain disagreeable ideas on the unsupported presumption that their very disagreeableness will provoke violence.

Thus, we have not permitted the Government to assume that every expression of a provocative idea will incite a riot, but have instead required careful consideration of the actual circumstances surrounding such expression, asking whether the expression "is directed to inciting or producing imminent lawless action and is likely to incite or produce such action." To accept Texas' arguments that it need only demonstrate "the potential for a breach of the peace," and that every flag-burning necessarily possesses that potential, would be to eviscerate our holding in *Brandenburg*. This we decline to do.

Nor does Johnson's expressive conduct fall within that ᴗmall class of "fighting words" that are "likely to provoke the average person to retaliation, and thereby cause a breach of the peace." No reasonable onlooker would have regarded Johnson's generalized expression of dissatisfaction with the policies of the Federal Government as a direct personal insult or an invitation to exchange fisticuffs.

We thus conclude that the State's interest in maintaining order is not implicated on these facts. The State need not worry that our holding will disable it from preserving the peace. We do not suggest that the First Amendment forbids a State to prevent "imminent lawless action." And, in fact, Texas already has a statute specifically prohibiting breaches of the peace, which tends to confirm that Texas need not punish this flag desecration in order to keep the peace.

The State also asserts an interest in preserving the flag as a symbol of nationhood and national unity. In *Spence*, we acknowledged that the Government's interest in preserving the flag's special symbolic value "is directly related to expression in the context of activity" such as affixing a peace symbol to a flag. We are equally persuaded that this interest is related to expression in the case of Johnson's burning of the flag. The State, apparently, is concerned that such conduct will lead people to believe either that the flag does not stand for nationhood and national unity, but instead reflects other, less positive concepts, or that the concepts reflected in the flag do not in fact exist, that is, we do not enjoy unity as a Nation. These concerns blossom only when a person's treatment of the flag communicates some message, and thus are related "to the suppression of free expression" within the meaning of *O'Brien.* We are thus outside of *O'Brien*'s test altogether.

It remains to consider whether the State's interest in preserving the flag as a symbol of nationhood and national unity justifies Johnson's conviction.

As in *Spence,* "[w]e are confronted with a case of prosecution for the expression of an idea through activity," and "[a]ccordingly, we must examine with particular care the interests advanced by [petitioner] to support its prosecution." Johnson was not, we add, prosecuted for the expression of just any idea; he was prosecuted for this expression of dissatisfaction with the policies of this country, expression situated at the core of our First Amendment values.

Moreover, Johnson was prosecuted because he knew that his politically charged expression would cause "serious offense." If he had burned the flag as a means of disposing of it because it was dirty or torn, he would not have been convicted of flag desecration under this Texas law: federal law designates burning as the preferred means of disposing of a flag "when it is in such condition that it is no longer a fitting emblem for display," and Texas has no quarrel with this means of disposal. The Texas law is thus not aimed at protecting the physical integrity of the flag in all circumstances, but is designed instead to protect it

only against impairments that would cause serious offense
to others.   Texas concedes as much: "Section 42.09(b)
reaches only those severe acts of physical abuse of the
flag carried out in a way likely to be offensive. The statute mandates intentional or knowing abuse, that is, the
kind of mistreatment that is not innocent, but rather is in-
tentionally designed to seriously offend other individuals."

Whether Johnson's treatment of the flag violated Texas
law thus depended on the likely communicative impact of
his expressive conduct. Our decision in *Boos v. Barry* tells
us that this restriction on Johnson's expression is content-
based. In *Boos*, we considered the constitutionality of a
law prohibiting "the display of any sign within 50 feet of
a foreign embassy if that sign tends to bring that foreign
government into 'public odium' or 'public disrepute.'"
Rejecting the argument that the law was content-neutral
because it was justified by "our international law obligation to shield diplomats from speech that offends their
dignity," we held that "[t]he emotive impact of speech on
its audience is not a 'secondary effect'" unrelated to the
content of the expression itself.

According to the principles announced in *Boos*, Johnson's
political expression was restricted because of the content
of the message he conveyed. We must therefore subject
the State's asserted interest in preserving the special symbolic character of the flag to "the most exacting scrutiny."

Texas argues that its interest in preserving the flag as a
symbol of nationhood and national unity survives this
close analysis. Quoting extensively from the writings of
this Court chronicling the flag's historic and symbolic role
in our society, the State emphasizes the "'special place'"
reserved for the flag in our Nation. The State's argument

is not that it has an interest simply in maintaining the flag as a symbol of *something*, no matter what it symbolizes; indeed, if that were the State's position, it would be difficult to see how that interest is endangered by highly symbolic conduct such as Johnson's. Rather, the State's claim is that it has an interest in preserving the flag as a symbol of *nationhood* and *national unity*, a symbol with a determinate range of meanings. According to Texas, if one physically treats the flag in a way that would tend to cast doubt on either the idea that nationhood and national unity are the flag's referents or that national unity actually exists, the message conveyed thereby is a harmful one and therefore may be prohibited.

If there is a bedrock principle underlying the First Amendment, it is that the Government may not prohibit the expression of an idea simply because society finds the idea itself offensive or disagreeable.

We have not recognized an exception to this principle even where our flag has been involved. In *Street v. New York* (1969), we held that a State may not criminally punish a person for uttering words critical of the flag. Rejecting the argument that the conviction could be sustained on the ground that Street had "failed to show the respect for our national symbol which may properly be demanded of every citizen," we concluded that "the constitutionally guaranteed 'freedom to be intellectually . . . diverse or even contrary,' and the 'right to differ as to things that touch the heart of the existing order,' encompass the freedom to express publicly one's opinions about our flag, including those opinions which are defiant or contemptuous." Nor may the Government, we have held, compel conduct that would evince respect for the flag. "To sustain the compulsory flag salute we are required to say that a Bill of Rights which guards the individual's right to speak his own mind, left it open to public authorities to compel him to utter what is not in his mind."

In holding in *Barnette* that the Constitution did not leave this course open to the Government, Justice Jackson described one of our society's defining principles in words deserving of their frequent repetition: "If there is any fixed star in our constitutional constellation, it is that no official, high or petty, can prescribe what shall be orthodox in politics, nationalism, religion, or other matters of opinion or force citizens to confess by word or act their faith therein." In *Spence*, we held that the same interest asserted by Texas here was insufficient to support a criminal conviction under a flag-misuse statute for the taping of a peace sign to an American flag. "Given the protected character of [Spence's] expression and in light of the fact that no interest the State may have in preserving the physical integrity of a privately owned flag was significantly impaired on these facts," we held, "the conviction must be invalidated."

In short, nothing in our precedents suggests that a State may foster its own view of the flag by prohibiting expressive conduct relating to it." To bring its argument outside our precedents, Texas attempts to convince us that even if its interest in preserving the flag's symbolic role does not allow it to prohibit words or some expressive conduct critical of the flag, it does permit it to forbid the outright destruction of the flag. The State's argument cannot depend here on the distinction between written or spoken words and nonverbal conduct. That distinction, we have shown, is of no moment where the nonverbal conduct is expressive, as it is here, and where the regulation of that conduct is related to expression, as it is here. In addition, both

Barnette and *Spence* involved expressive conduct, not only verbal communication, and both found that conduct protected.

Texas' focus on the precise nature of Johnson's expression, moreover, misses the point of our prior decisions: their enduring lesson, that the Government may not prohibit expression simply because it disagrees with its message, is not dependent on the particular mode in which one chooses to express an idea. If we were to hold that a State may forbid flag-burning wherever it is likely to endanger the flag's symbolic role, but allow it wherever burning a flag promotes that role - as where, for example, a person ceremoniously burns a dirty flag - we would be saying that when it comes to impairing the flag's physical integrity, the flag itself may be used as a symbol - as a substitute for the written or spoken word or a "short cut from mind to mind" - only in one direction. We would be permitting a State to "prescribe what shall be orthodox" by saying that one may burn the flag to convey one's attitude toward it and its referents only if one does not endanger the flag's representation of nationhood and national unity.

We never before have held that the Government may assure that a symbol be used to express only one view of that symbol or its referents. Indeed, in *Schacht v. United States*, we invalidated a federal statute permitting an actor portraying a member of one of our armed forces to "'wear the uniform of that armed force if the portrayal does not tend to discredit that armed force.'" This proviso, we held, "which leaves Americans free to praise the war in Vietnam but can send persons like Schacht to prison for opposing it, cannot survive in a country which has the First Amendment."

We perceive no basis on which to hold that the principle underlying our decision in *Schacht* does not apply to this case. To conclude that the Government may permit designated symbols to be used to communicate only a limited set of messages would be to enter territory having no discernible or defensible boundaries. Could the Government, on this theory, prohibit the burning of state flags? Of copies of the Presidential seal? Of the Constitution? In evaluating these choices under the First Amendment, how would we decide which symbols were sufficiently special to warrant this unique status? To do so, we would be forced to consult our own political preferences, and impose them on the citizenry, in the very way that the First Amendment forbids us to do.

There is, moreover, no indication - either in the text of the Constitution or in our cases interpreting it - that a separate juridical category exists for the American flag alone. Indeed, we would not be surprised to learn that the persons who framed our Constitution and wrote the Amendment that we now construe were not known for their reverence for the Union Jack. The First Amendment does not guarantee that other concepts virtually sacred to our Nation as a whole - such as the principle that discrimination on the basis of race is odious and destructive - will go unquestioned in the marketplace of ideas. We decline, therefore, to create for the flag an exception to the joust of principles protected by the First Amendment.

It is not the State's ends, but its means, to which we object. It cannot be gainsaid that there is a special place reserved for the flag in this Nation, and thus we do not doubt that the Government has a legitimate interest in

making efforts to "preserv[e] the national flag as an unal-
loyed symbol of our country." We reject the suggestion,
urged at oral argument by counsel for Johnson, that the
Government lacks "any state interest whatsoever" in regulating the manner in which the flag may be displayed.
Congress has, for example, enacted . . . regulations describing the proper treatment of the flag, and we cast no doubt
on the legitimacy of its interest in making such recommendations. To say that the Government has an interest
in encouraging proper treatment of the flag, however, is
not to say that it may criminally punish a person for
burning a flag as a means of political protest. "National
unity as an end which officials may foster by persuasion
and example is not in question. The problem is whether
under our Constitution compulsion as here employed is a
permissible means for its achievement."

We are fortified in today's conclusion by our conviction
that forbidding criminal punishment for conduct such as
Johnson's will not endanger the special role played by our
flag or the feelings it inspires. To paraphrase Justice
Holmes, we submit that nobody can suppose that this one
gesture of an unknown man will change our Nation's attitude towards its flag. Indeed, Texas' argument that the
burning of an American flag "'is an act having a high
likelihood to cause a breach of the peace,'" and its
statute's implicit assumption that physical mistreatment
of the flag will lead to "serious offense," tend to confirm
that the flag's special role is not in danger; if it were, no
one would riot or take offense because a flag had been
burned.

We are tempted to say, in fact, that the flag's deservedly
cherished place in our community will be strengthened,
not weakened, by our holding today. Our decision is a re-

affirmation of the principles of freedom and inclusiveness that the flag best reflects, and of the conviction that our toleration of criticism such as Johnson's is a sign and source of our strength.   Indeed, one of the proudest images of our flag, the one immortalized in our own national anthem, is of the bombardment it survived at Fort McHenry.   It is the Nation's resilience, not its rigidity, that Texas sees reflected in the flag - and it is that resilience that we reassert today.

The way to preserve the flag's special role is not to punish those who feel differently about these matters.   It is to persuade them that they are wrong. "To courageous, self-reliant men, with confidence in the power of free and fearless reasoning applied through the processes of popular government, no danger flowing from speech can be deemed clear and present, unless the incidence of the evil apprehended is so imminent that it may befall before there is opportunity for full discussion. If there be time to expose through discussion the falsehood and fallacies, to avert the evil by the processes of education, the remedy to be applied is more speech, not enforced silence." And, precisely because it is our flag that is involved, one's response to the flag-burner may exploit the uniquely persuasive power of the flag itself. We can imagine no more appropriate response to burning a flag than waving one's own, no better way to counter a flag-burner's message than by saluting the flag that burns, no surer means of preserving the dignity even of the flag that burned than by - as one witness here did - according its remains a respectful burial. We do not consecrate the flag by punishing its desecration, for in doing so we dilute the freedom that this cherished emblem represents.

Johnson was convicted for engaging in expressive conduct. The State's interest in preventing breaches of the peace does not support his conviction because Johnson's conduct did not threaten to disturb the peace. Nor does the State's interest in preserving the flag as a symbol of nationhood and national unity justify his criminal conviction for engaging in political expression. The judgment of the Texas Court of Criminal Appeals is therefore *Affirmed.*

THE U.S. CONSTITUTION

THE U.S. CONSTITUTION

PREAMBLE

We the people of the United States, in order to form a more perfect union, establish justice, insure domestic tranquility, provide for the common defense, promote the general welfare, and secure the blessings of liberty to ourselves and our posterity, do ordain and establish this Constitution for the United States of America.

ARTICLE I

Section 1. All legislative powers herein granted shall be vested in a Congress of the United States, which shall consist of a Senate and House of Representatives.

Section 2. (1) The House of Representatives shall be composed of members chosen every second year by the people of the several states, and the electors in each state shall have the qualifications requisite for electors of the most numerous branch of the State Legislature.

(2) No person shall be a Representative who shall not have attained to the age of twenty-five years, and been seven years a citizen of the United States, and who shall not, when elected, be an inhabitant of that state in which he shall be chosen.

(3) Representatives and direct taxes shall be apportioned among the several states which may be included within this union, according to their respective numbers, which shall be determined by adding to the whole number of free persons, including those bound to service for a term of years, and excluding Indians not taxed, three-fifths of all other persons. The actual enumeration shall be made

within three years after the first meeting of the Congress
of the United States, and within every subsequent term of
ten years, in such manner as they shall by law direct. The
number of Representatives shall not exceed one for every
thirty thousand, but each state shall have at least one Representative; and until such enumeration shall be made, the
State of New Hampshire shall be entitled to choose three,
Massachusetts eight, Rhode Island and Providence Planta-
tions one, Connecticut five, New York six, New Jersey
four, Pennsylvania eight, Delaware one, Maryland six, Virginia ten, North Carolina five, South Carolina five, and
Georgia three.

(4) When vacancies happen in the representation from
any state, the executive authority thereof shall issue writs
of election to fill such vacancies.

(5) The House of Representatives shall choose their
Speaker and other Officers; and shall have the sole power
of impeachment.

Section 3. (1) The Senate of the United States shall be
composed of two Senators from each state, chosen by the
legislature thereof, for six years; and each Senator shall
have one vote.

(2) Immediately after they shall be assembled in consequence of the first election, they shall be divided as equally as may be into three classes. The seats of the Senators
of the first class shall be vacated at the expiration of the
second year, of the second class at the expiration of the
fourth year, and of the third class at the expiration of the
sixth year, so that one-third may be chosen every second
year; and if vacancies happen by resignation, or otherwise,
during the recess of the legislature of any state, the execu-

tive thereof may make temporary appointments until the next meeting of the legislature, which shall then fill such vacancies.

(3) No person shall be a Senator who shall not have attained to the age of thirty years, and been nine years a citizen of the United States, and who shall not, when elected, be an inhabitant of that state for which he shall be chosen.

(4) The Vice President of the United States shall be President of the Senate, but shall have no vote, unless they be equally divided.

(5) The Senate shall choose their other Officers, and also a President pro tempore, in the absence of the Vice President, or when he shall exercise the Office of President of the United States.

(6) The Senate shall have the sole power to try all impeachments. When sitting for that purpose, they shall be on oath or affirmation. When the President of the United States is tried, the Chief Justice shall preside: and no person shall be convicted without the concurrence of two-thirds of the members present.

(7) Judgment in cases of impeachment shall not extend further than to removal from office, and disqualification to hold and enjoy any office of honor, trust, or profit under the United States: but the party convicted shall nevertheless be liable and subject to indictment, trial, judgment, and punishment, according to law.

Section 4. (1) The times, places and manner of holding elections for Senators and Representatives, shall be pre-

scribed in each state by the legislature thereof; but the
Congress may at any time by law make or alter such regulations, except as to the places of choosing Senators.

(2) The Congress shall assemble at least once in every
year, and such meeting shall be on the first Monday in
December, unless they shall by law appoint a different
day.

Section 5. (1) Each House shall be the judge of the elections, returns, and qualifications of its own members, and
a majority of each shall constitute a quorum to do business; but a smaller number may adjourn from day to day,
and may be authorized to compel the attendance of absent
members, in such manner, and under such penalties as
each House may provide.

(2) Each House may determine the rules of its proceedings, punish its members for disorderly behavior, and,
with the concurrence of two-thirds, expel a member.

(3) Each House shall keep a journal of its proceedings,
and from time to time publish the same, excepting such
parts as may in their judgment require secrecy; and the
yeas and nays of the members of either House on any
question shall, at the desire of one-fifth of those present,
be entered on the journal.

(4) Neither House, during the Session of Congress, shall,
without the consent of the other, adjourn for more than
three days, nor to any other place than that in which the
two Houses shall be sitting.

Section 6. (1) The Senators and Representatives shall receive a compensation for their services, to be ascertained

by law, and paid out of the Treasury of the United States. They shall in all cases, except treason, felony and breach of the peace, be privileged from arrest during their attendance at the session of their respective Houses, and in going to and returning from the same; and for any speech or debate in either House, they shall not be questioned in any other place.

(2) No Senator or Representative shall, during the time for which he was elected, be appointed to any civil office under the authority of the United States, which shall have been created, or the emoluments whereof shall have been increased during such time and no person holding any office under the United States, shall be a member of either House during his continuance in office.

Section 7. (1) All bills for raising revenue shall originate in the House of Representatives; but the Senate may propose or concur with amendments as on other bills.

(2) Every bill which shall have passed the House of Representatives and the Senate, shall, before it become a law, be presented to the President of the United States; if he approve he shall sign it, but if not he shall return it, with his objections to the House in which it shall have originated, who shall enter the objections at large on their journal, and proceed to reconsider it. If after such reconsideration two-thirds of that House shall agree to pass the bill, it shall be sent together with the objections, to the other House, by which it shall likewise be reconsidered, and if approved by two-thirds of that House, it shall become a law. But in all such cases the votes of both Houses shall be determined by yeas and nays, and the names of the persons voting for and against the bill shall be entered on the journal of each House respectively. If any bill shall not

be returned by the President within ten days (Sundays excepted) after it shall have been presented to him, the same shall be a law, in like manner as if he had signed it, unless the Congress by their adjournment prevent its return in which case it shall not be a law.

(3) Every order, resolution, or vote, to which the concurrence of the Senate and House of Representatives may be necessary (except on a question of adjournment) shall be presented to the President of the United States; and before the same shall take effect, shall be approved by him, or being disapproved by him, shall be repassed by two-thirds of the Senate and House of Representatives, according to the rules and limitations prescribed in the case of a bill.

Section 8. (1) The Congress shall have the power to lay and collect taxes, duties, imposts and excises, to pay the debts and provide for the common defense and general welfare of the United States; but all duties, imposts and excises shall be uniform throughout the United States;

(2) To borrow money on the credit of the United States;

(3) To regulate commerce with foreign nations, and among the several states, and with the Indian Tribes;

(4) To establish an uniform Rule of Naturalization, and uniform laws on the subject of bankruptcies throughout the United States;

(5) To coin money, regulate the value thereof, and of foreign coin, and fix the standard of weights and measures;

(6) To provide for the punishment of counterfeiting the securities and current coin of the United States;

(7) To establish Post Offices and Post Roads;

(8) To promote the progress of science and useful arts, by securing for limited times to authors and inventors the exclusive right to their respective writings and discoveries;

(9) To constitute tribunals inferior to the Supreme Court;

(10) To define and punish piracies and felonies committed on the high seas, and offenses against the Law of Nations;

(11) To declare war, grant Letters of marque and reprisal, and make rules concerning captures on land and water;

(12) To raise and support armies, but no appropriation of money to that use shall be for a longer term than two years;

(13) To provide and maintain a Navy;

(14) To make rules for the government and regulation of the land and naval forces;

(15) To provide for calling forth the Militia to execute the laws of the Union, suppress insurrections and repel invasions;

(16) To provide for organizing, arming, and disciplining, the Militia, and for governing such part of them as may be employed in the service of the United States, reserving to the states respectively, the appointment of the Officers,

and the authority of training the Militia according to the discipline prescribed by Congress;

(17) To exercise exclusive legislation in all cases whatsoever, over such district (not exceeding ten miles square) as may, by cession of particular states, and the acceptance of Congress, become the Seat of the Government of the United States, and to exercise like authority over all places purchased by the consent of the legislature of the state in which the same shall be, for the erection of forts, magazines, arsenals, dockyards, and other needful buildings; - and

(18) To make all laws which shall be necessary and proper for carrying into execution the foregoing powers, and all other powers vested by this Constitution in the Government of the United States, or in any Department or Officer thereof.

Section 9. (1) The migration or importation of such persons as any of the states now existing shall think proper to admit, shall not be prohibited by the Congress prior to the year one thousand eight hundred and eight, but a tax or duty may be imposed on such importation, not exceeding ten dollars for each person.

(2) The privilege of the writ of habeas corpus shall not be suspended, unless when in cases of rebellion or invasion the public safety may require it.

(3) No bill of attainder or ex post facto law shall be passed.

(4) No capitation, or other direct, tax shall be laid, unless in proportion to the census or enumeration herein before directed to be taken.

(5) No tax or duty shall be laid on articles exported from any state.

(6) No preference shall be given by any regulation of commerce or revenue to the ports of one state over those of another: nor shall vessels bound to, or from, one state be obliged to enter, clear, or pay duties in another.

(7) No money shall be drawn from the Treasury, but in consequence of appropriations made by law; and a regular statement and account of the receipts and expenditures of all public money shall be published from time to time.

(8) No title of nobility shall be granted by the United States: and no person holding any office of profit or trust under them, shall, without the consent of the Congress, accept of any present, emolument, office, or title, of any kind whatever, from any King, Prince, or foreign State.

Section 10. (1) No state shall enter into any treaty, alliance, or confederation; grant letters of marque and reprisal; coin money; emit bills of credit; make any thing but gold and silver coin a tender in payment of debts; pass any bill of attainder, ex post facto law, or law impairing the obligation of contracts, or grant any title of nobility.

(2) No state shall, without the consent of the Congress, lay any imposts or duties on imports or exports, except what may be absolutely necessary for executing its inspection laws: and the net produce of all duties and imposts, laid by any state on imports or exports, shall be for the use of

the Treasury of the United States; and all such laws shall be subject to the revision and control of the Congress.

(3) No state shall, without the consent of Congress, lay any duty of tonnage, keep troops, or ships of war in time of peace, enter into any agreement or compact with another state, or with a foreign power, or engage in war, unless actually invaded, or in such imminent danger as will not admit of delay.

ARTICLE II

Section 1. (1) The executive power shall be vested in a President of the United States of America. He shall hold his office during the term of four years, and, together with the Vice President, chosen for the same term, be elected, as follows:

(2) Each state shall appoint, in such manner as the legislature thereof may direct, a number of electors, equal to the whole number of Senators and Representatives to which the state may be entitled in the Congress; but no Senator or Representative, or person holding an office of trust or profit under the United States, shall be appointed an Elector.

(3) The electors shall meet in their respective states, and vote by ballot for two persons, of whom one at least shall not be an inhabitant of the same state with themselves. And they shall make a list of all the persons voted for, and of the number of votes for each; which list they shall sign and certify, and transmit sealed to the Seat of the Government of the United States, directed to the President of the Senate. The President of the Senate shall, in the presence of the Senate and House of Representatives,

open all the certificates, and the votes shall then be counted. The person having the greatest number of votes shall be the President, if such number be a majority of the whole number of electors appointed; and if there be more than one who have such majority, and have an equal number of votes, then the House of Representatives shall immediately choose by ballot one of them for President; and if no person have a majority, then from the five highest on the list the said House shall in like manner choose the President. But in choosing the President, the votes shall be taken by states the representation from each state having one vote; a quorum for this purpose shall consist of a member or members from two-thirds of the states, and a majority of all the states shall be necessary to a choice. In every case, after the choice of the President, the person having the greater number of votes of the electors shall be the Vice President. But if there should remain two or more who have equal votes, the Senate shall choose from them by ballot the Vice President.

(4) The Congress may determine the time of choosing the Electors, and the day on which they shall give their votes; which day shall be the same throughout the United States.

(5) No person except a natural born citizen, or a citizen of the United States, at the time of the adoption of this Constitution, shall be eligible to the Office of President; neither shall any person be eligible to that Office who shall not have attained to the age of thirty-five years, and been fourteen years a resident within the United States.

(6) In case of the removal of the President from Office, or of his death, resignation or inability to discharge the powers and duties of the said Office, the same shall devolve on the Vice President, and the Congress may by law

provide for the case of removal, death, resignation or inability, both of the President and Vice President, declaring
what Officer shall then act as President, and such Officer
shall act accordingly, until the disability be removed, or a
President shall be elected.

(7) The President shall, at stated times, receive for his
services, a compensation, which shall neither be increased
nor diminished during the period for which he shall have
been elected, and he shall not receive within that period
any other emolument from the United States, or any of
them.

(8) Before he enter on the execution of his office, he shall
take the following oath or affirmation: "I do solemnly
swear (or affirm) that I will faithfully execute the Office
of President of the United States, and will to the best of
my ability, preserve, protect and defend the Constitution
of the United States."

Section 2. (1) The President shall be Commander in Chief
of the Army and Navy of the United States, and of the
militia of the several states, when called into the actual
service of the United States; he may require the opinion,
in writing, of the principal Officer in each of the Executive Departments, upon any subject relating to the duties
of their respective Offices, and he shall have power to
grant reprieves and pardons for offenses against the United States, except in cases of impeachment.

(2) He shall have power, by and with the advice and consent of the Senate to make treaties, provided two-thirds of
the Senators present concur; and he shall nominate, and
by and with the advice and consent of the Senate, shall appoint Ambassadors, other public Ministers and Consuls,

Judges of the supreme Court, and all other Officers of the United States, whose appointments are not herein otherwise provided for, and which shall be established by law; but the Congress may by law vest the appointment of such inferior Officers, as they think proper, in the President alone, in the courts of law, or in the heads of departments.

(3) The President shall have power to fill up all vacancies that may happen during the recess of the Senate, by granting commissions which shall expire at the end of their next session.

Section 3. He shall from time to time give to the Congress information of the State of the Union, and recommend to their consideration such measures as he shall judge necessary and expedient; he may, on extraordinary occasions, convene both Houses, or either of them, and in case of disagreement between them, with respect to the time of adjournment, he may adjourn them to such time as he shall think proper; he shall receive Ambassadors and other public Ministers; he shall take care that the laws be faithfully executed, and shall commission all the Officers of the United States.

Section 4. The President, Vice President and all civil Officers of the United States, shall be removed from office on impeachment for, and conviction of, treason, bribery, or other high crimes and misdemeanors.

ARTICLE III

Section 1. The judicial power of the United States, shall be vested in one supreme Court, and in such inferior courts as the Congress may from time to time ordain and establish. The Judges, both of the supreme and inferior courts, shall hold their Offices during good behaviour, and shall, at stated times, receive for their services a compensation, which shall not be diminished during their continuance in office.

Section 2. (1) The judicial power shall extend to all cases, in law and equity, arising under this Constitution, the laws of the United States, and treaties made, or which shall be made, under their authority; - to all cases affecting Ambassadors, other public Ministers and Consuls; - to all cases of admiralty and maritime jurisdiction; - to controversies to which the United States shall be a party; - to controversies between two or more states; - between a state and citizens of another state; - between citizens of different states; - between citizens of the same state claiming lands under the grants of different states, and between a state, or the citizens thereof, and foreign states, citizens or subjects.

(2) In all cases affecting Ambassadors, other public Ministers and Consuls, and those in which a state shall be a party, the supreme Court shall have original jurisdiction. In all the other cases before mentioned, the supreme Court shall have appellate jurisdiction, both as to law and fact, with such exceptions, and under such regulations as the Congress shall make.

(3) The trial of all crimes, except in cases of impeachment, shall be by jury; and such trial shall be held in the state where the said crimes shall have been committed; but when not committed within any state, the trial shall be at such place or places as the Congress may by law have directed.

Section 3. (1) Treason against the United States, shall consist only in levying war against them, or, in adhering to their enemies, giving them aid and comfort. No person shall be convicted of treason unless on the testimony of two witnesses to the same overt act, or on confession in open Court.

(2) The Congress shall have power to declare the punishment of treason, but no Attainder of Treason shall work corruption of blood, or forfeiture except during the life of the person attainted.

ARTICLE IV

Section 1. Full faith and credit shall be given in each state to the public acts, records, and judicial proceedings of every other state. And the Congress may by general laws prescribe the manner in which such acts, records and proceedings shall be proved, and the effect thereof.

Section 2. (1) The citizens of each state shall be entitled to all privileges and immunities of citizens in the several states.

(2) A person charged in any state with treason, felony, or other crime, who shall flee from justice, and be found in another state, shall on demand of the executive authority of the state from which he fled, be delivered up, to be removed to the state having jurisdiction of the crime.

(3) No person held to service or labor in one state, under the laws thereof, escaping into another, shall, in consequence of any law or regulation therein, be discharged from such service or labor, but shall be delivered up on

claim of the party to whom such service or labor may be due.

Section 3. (1) New states may be admitted by the Congress into this union; but no new state shall be formed or erected within the jurisdiction of any other state; nor any state be formed by the junction of two or more states, or parts of states, without the consent of the legislatures of the states concerned as well as of the Congress.

(2) The Congress shall have power to dispose of and make all needful rules and regulations respecting the territory or other property belonging to the United States; and nothing in this Constitution shall be so construed as to prejudice any claims of the United States, or of any particular state.

Section 4. The United States shall guarantee to every state in this union a Republican form of government, and shall protect each of them against invasion; and on application of the legislature, or of the executive (when the legislature cannot be convened) against domestic violence.

ARTICLE V

The Congress, whenever two-thirds of both Houses shall deem it necessary, shall propose amendments to this Constitution, or, on the application of the legislatures of two-thirds of the several states, shall call a convention for proposing amendments, which, in either case, shall be valid to all intents and purposes, as part of this constitution, when ratified by the legislatures of three-fourths of the several states, or by conventions in three-fourths thereof, as the one or the other mode of ratification may be proposed by the Congress; provided that no amendment which may be made prior to the year one thousand eight hundred and eight shall in any manner affect the first and fourth clauses in the Ninth Section of the first Article; and that no state, without its consent, shall be deprived of its equal suffrage in the Senate.

ARTICLE VI

(1) All debts contracted and engagements entered into, before the adoption of this Constitution shall be as valid against the United States under this Constitution, as under the Confederation.

(2) This Constitution, and the laws of the United States which shall be made in pursuance thereof; and all treaties made, or which shall be made, under the authority of the United States, shall be the supreme law of the land; and the Judges in every state shall be bound thereby, any thing in the Constitution or laws of any state to the contrary notwithstanding.

(3) The Senators and Representatives before mentioned, and the Members of the several State Legislatures, and all executive and judicial Officers, both of the United States and of the several states, shall be bound by oath or affirmation, to support this Constitution; but no religious test shall ever be required as a qualification to any office or public trust under the United States.

ARTICLE VII

The ratification of the Conventions of nine states shall be sufficient for the establishment of this Constitution between the states so ratifying the same.

AMENDMENT I (1791)

Congress shall make no law respecting an establishment of religion, or prohibiting the free exercise thereof; or abridging the freedom of speech, or of the press; or the right of the people peaceably to assemble, and to petition the Government for a redress of grievances.

AMENDMENT II (1791)

A well regulated Militia, being necessary to the security of a free state, the right of the people to keep and bear arms, shall not be infringed.

AMENDMENT III (1791)

No soldier shall, in time of peace be quartered in any house, without the consent of the owner, nor in time of war, but in a manner to be prescribed by law.

AMENDMENT IV (1791)

The right of the people to be secure in their persons, houses, papers, and effects, against unreasonable searches and seizures, shall not be violated, and no warrants shall issue, but upon probable cause, supported by oath or affirmation, and particularly describing the place to be searched, and the persons or things to be seized.

AMENDMENT V (1791)

No person shall be held to answer for a capital, or otherwise infamous crime, unless on a presentment or indictment of a Grand Jury, except in cases arising in the land or naval forces, or in the Militia, when in actual service in time of war or public danger; nor shall any person be subject for the same offense to be twice put in jeopardy of life or limb; nor shall be compelled in any criminal case to be a witness against himself, nor be deprived of life, liberty, or property, without due process of law; nor shall private property be taken for public use, without just compensation.

AMENDMENT VI (1791)

In all criminal prosecutions, the accused shall enjoy the right to a speedy and public trial, by an impartial jury of the state and district wherein the crime shall have been committed, which district shall have been previously ascertained by law, and to be informed of the nature and cause of the accusation; to be confronted with the witnesses against him; to have compulsory process for obtaining witnesses in his favor, and to have the assistance of counsel for his defense.

AMENDMENT VII (1791)

In suits at common law, where the value in controversy shall exceed twenty dollars, the right of trial by jury shall be preserved, and no fact tried by jury, shall be otherwise re-examined in any court of the United States, than according to the rules of the common law.

AMENDMENT VIII (1791)

Excessive bail shall not be required, nor excessive fines imposed, nor cruel and unusual punishments inflicted.

AMENDMENT IX (1791)

The enumeration in the Constitution, of certain rights, shall not be construed to deny or disparage others retained by the people.

AMENDMENT X (1791)

The powers not delegated to the United States by the Constitution, nor prohibited by it to the States, are reserved to the States respectively, or to the people.

AMENDMENT XI (1798)

The judicial power of the United States shall not be construed to extend to any suit in law or equity, commenced or prosecuted against one of the United States by citizens of another state, or by citizens or subjects of any foreign state.

AMENDMENT XII (1804)

The Electors shall meet in their respective states and vote by ballot for President and Vice-President, one of whom, at least, shall not be an inhabitant of the same state with themselves; they shall name in their ballots the person voted for as President, and in distinct ballots the person voted for as Vice-President, and they shall make distinct lists of all persons voted for as President, and of all persons voted for as Vice-President, and of the number of votes for each, which lists they shall sign and certify, and transmit sealed to the seat of the government of the United States, directed to the President of the Senate; - the President of the Senate shall, in the presence of the Senate and House of Representatives, open all the certificates and the votes shall then be counted; - the person having the greatest number of votes for President, shall be the President, if such number be a majority of the whole number of electors appointed; and if no person have such majority, then from the persons having the highest numbers not exceeding three on the list of those voted for as President, the House of Representatives shall choose immediately, by ballot, the President. But in choosing the President, the votes shall be taken by states, the representation from each state having one vote; a quorum for this purpose shall consist of a member or members from two-thirds of the states, and a majority of all the states shall be necessary to a choice. And if the House of Representatives shall not choose a President whenever the right of choice shall devolve upon them before the fourth day of March next following, then the Vice-President shall act as President, as in the case of the death or other constitutional disability of the President. - The person having the greatest number of votes as Vice-President, shall be the Vice-President, if such number be a majority of the whole number of Electors appointed, and if no person have a majority, then from the two highest numbers on the list, the Senate shall choose the Vice-President; a quorum for the purpose shall consist of two-thirds of the whole number of Senators, and a majority of the whole number shall be necessary to a choice. But no person constitutionally ineligible to the office of President shall be eligible to that of Vice-President of the United States.

AMENDMENT XIII (1865)

Section 1. Neither slavery nor involuntary servitude, except as a punishment for crime whereof the party shall have been duly convicted, shall exist within the United States, or any place subject to their jurisdiction.

Section 2. Congress shall have power to enforce this article by appropriate legislation.

AMENDMENT XIV (1868)

Section 1. All persons born or naturalized in the United States, and subject to the jurisdiction thereof, are citizens of the United States and of the state wherein they reside. No state shall make or enforce any law which shall abridge the privileges or immunities of citizens of the United States; nor shall any state deprive any person of life, liberty, or property, without due process of law; nor deny to any person within its jurisdiction the equal protection of the laws.

Section 2. Representatives shall be apportioned among the several states according to their respective numbers, counting the whole number of persons in each State excluding Indians not taxed. But when the right to vote at any election for the choice of electors for President and Vice President of the United States, Representatives in Congress, the Executive and Judicial officers of a state, or the members of the Legislature thereof, is denied to any of the male inhabitants of such state, being twenty-one years of age, and citizens of the United States, or in any way abridged, except for participation in rebellion, or other crime, the basis of representation therein shall be reduced in the proportion which the number of such male citizens shall bear to the whole number of male citizens twenty-one years of age in such state.

Section 3. No person shall be a Senator or Representative in Congress, or elector of President and Vice President, or hold any office, civil or military, under the United States, or under any state, who having previously taken an oath, as a member of Congress, or as an officer of the United States, or as a member of any state legislature, or as an executive or judicial officer of any state, to support the Constitution of the United States, shall have engaged in insurrection or rebellion against the same, or given aid or comfort to the enemies thereof. But Congress may by a vote of two-thirds of each House, remove such disability.

Section 4. The validity of the public debt of the United States, authorized by law, including debts incurred for payment of pensions and bounties for services in suppressing insurrection or rebellion, shall not be questioned. But neither the United States nor any state shall assume or pay any debt or obligation incurred in aid of insurrection or rebellion against the United States, or any claim for the loss or emancipation of any slave; but all such debts, obligations and claims shall be held illegal and void.

Section 5. The Congress shall have power to enforce, by appropriate legislation, the provisions of this article.

AMENDMENT XV (1870)

Section 1. The right of citizens of the United States to vote shall not be denied or abridged by the United States or by any state on account of race, color, or previous condition of servitude.

Section 2. The Congress shall have power to enforce this article by appropriate legislation.

AMENDMENT XVI (1913)

The Congress shall have power to lay and collect taxes on incomes, from whatever source derived, without apportionment among the several states, and without regard to any census or enumeration.

AMENDMENT XVII (1913)

(1) The Senate of the United States shall be composed of two Senators from each state, elected by the people thereof, for six years; and each Senator shall have one vote. The electors in each State shall have the qualifications requisite for electors of the most numerous branch of the state legislatures.

(2) When vacancies happen in the representation of any state in the Senate, the executive authority of such state shall issue writs of election to fill such vacancies: *provided,* that the legislature of any state may empower the executive thereof to make temporary appointments until the people fill the vacancies by election as the legislature may direct.

(3) This amendment shall not be so construed as to affect the election or term of any Senator chosen before it becomes valid as part of the Constitution.

AMENDMENT XVIII (1919)

Section 1. After one year from the ratification of this article the manufacture, sale, or transportation of intoxicating liquors within, the importation thereof into, or the exportation thereof from the United States and all territory subject to the jurisdiction thereof for beverage purposes is hereby prohibited.

Section 2. The Congress and the several states shall have concurrent power to enforce this article by appropriate legislation.

Section 3. This article shall be inoperative unless it shall have been ratified as an amendment to the Constitution by the legislatures of the several states, as provided in the Constitution, within seven years from the date of the submission hereof to the states by the Congress.

AMENDMENT XIX (1920)

(1) The right of citizens of the United States to vote shall not be denied or abridged by the United States or by any state on account of sex.

(2) Congress shall have power to enforce this article by appropriate legislation.

AMENDMENT XX (1933)

Section 1. The terms of the President and Vice President shall end at noon on the 20th day of January, and the terms of Senators and Representatives at noon on the 3d day of January, of the years in which such terms would have ended if this article had not been ratified; and the terms of their successors shall then begin.

Section 2. The Congress shall assemble at least once in every year, and such meeting shall begin at noon on the 3d day of January, unless they shall by law appoint a different day.

Section 3. If, at the time fixed for the beginning of the term of the President, the President elect shall have died, the Vice President elect shall become President. If the President shall not have been chosen before the time fixed for the beginning of his term, or if the President elect shall have failed to qualify, then the Vice President elect shall act as President until a President shall have qualified; and the Congress may by law provide for the case wherein neither a President elect nor a Vice President elect shall have qualified, declaring who shall then act as President, or the manner in which one who is to act shall be selected, and such person shall act accordingly until a President or Vice President shall have qualified.

Section 4. The Congress may by law provide for the case of the death of any of the persons from whom the House of Representatives may choose a President whenever the right of choice shall have devolved upon them, and for the case of the death of any of the persons from whom the Senate may choose a Vice President whenever the right of choice shall have devolved upon them.

Section 5. Sections 1 and 2 shall take effect on the 15th day of October following the ratification of this article.

Section 6. This article shall be inoperative unless it shall have been ratified as an amendment to the Constitution by the legislatures of three-fourths of the several states within seven years from the date of its submission.

AMENDMENT XXI (1933)

Section 1. The eighteenth article of amendment to the Constitution of the United States is hereby repealed.

Section 2. The transportation or importation into any state, territory, or possession of the United States for delivery or use therein of intoxicating liquors, in violation of the laws thereof, is hereby prohibited.

Section 3. This article shall be inoperative unless it shall have been ratified as an amendment to the Constitution by conventions in the several states, as provided in the Constitution, within seven years from the date of the submission hereof to the states by the Congress.

AMENDMENT XXII (1951)

Section 1. No person shall be elected to the office of the President more than twice, and no person who has held the office of President, or acted as President, for more than two years of a term to which some other person was elected President shall be elected to the office of President more than once. But this Article shall not apply to any person holding the office of President when this Article was proposed by the Congress, and shall not prevent any person who may be holding the office of President, or acting as President, during the term within which this Article becomes operative from holding the office of President or acting as President during the remainder of such term.

Section 2. This article shall be inoperative unless it shall have been ratified as an amendment to the Constitution by the legislatures of three-fourths of the several states within seven years from the date of its submission to the states by the Congress.

AMENDMENT XXIII (1961)

Section 1. The District constituting the seat of Government of the United States shall appoint in such manner as the Congress may direct:

A number of electors of President and Vice President equal to the whole number of Senators and Representatives in Congress to which the District would be entitled if it were a state, but in no event more than the least populous state; they shall be in addition to those appointed by the states, but they shall be considered, for the purposes of the election of President and Vice President, to be electors appointed by a state; and they shall meet in the District and perform such duties as provided by the twelfth article of amendment.

Section 2. The Congress shall have power to enforce this article by appropriate legislation.

AMENDMENT XXIV (1964)

Section 1. The right of citizens of the United States to vote in any primary or other election for President or Vice President, for electors for President or Vice President, or for Senator or Representative in Congress, shall not be denied or abridged by the United States, or any state by reason of failure to pay any poll tax or other tax.

Section 2. The Congress shall have power to enforce this article by appropriate legislation.

AMENDMENT XXV (1967)

Section 1. In case of the removal of the President from office or of his death or resignation, the Vice President shall become President.

Section 2. Whenever there is a vacancy in the office of the Vice President, the President shall nominate a Vice President who shall take office upon confirmation by a majority vote of both Houses of Congress.

Section 3. Whenever the President transmits to the President pro tempore of the Senate and the Speaker of the House of Representatives his written declaration that he is unable to discharge the powers and duties of his office, and until he transmits to them a written declaration to the contrary, such powers and duties shall be discharged by the Vice President as Acting President.

Section 4. Whenever the Vice President and a majority of either the principal officers of the executive departments or of such other body as Congress may by law provide, transmit to the President pro tempore of the Senate and the Speaker of the House of Representatives their written declaration that the President is unable to discharge the powers and duties of his office, the Vice President shall immediately assume the powers and duties of the office as Acting President.

Thereafter, when the President transmits to the President pro tempore of the Senate and the Speaker of the House of Representatives his written declaration that no inability exists, he shall resume the powers and duties of his office unless the Vice President and a majority of either the principal officers of the executive department or of such other body as Congress may by law provide, transmit within four days to the President pro tempore of the Senate and the Speaker of the House of Representatives their written declaration and the President is unable to discharge the powers and duties of his office. Thereupon Congress shall decide the issue, assembling within forty-eight hours for that purpose if not in session. If the Congress, within twenty-one days after receipt of the latter written declaration, or, if Congress is not in session, within twenty-one days after Congress is required to assemble, determines by two-thirds vote of both Houses that the President is unable to discharge the power and duties of his office, the Vice President shall continue to discharge the same as Acting President; otherwise, the President shall resume the powers and duties of his office.

AMENDMENT XXVI (1971)

Section 1. The right of citizens of the United States, who are eighteen years of age or older, to vote shall not be denied or abridged by the United States or by any state on account of age.

Section 2. The Congress shall have power to enforce this article by appropriate legislation.

BIBLIOGRAPHY

Agresto, John, *The Supreme Court and Constitutional Democracy*, Ithaca: Cornell University Press, 1984.

Anthony, Lewis, *Clarence Earl Gideon and the Supreme Court*, New York: Random House, 1972.

Faux, Marian, *Roe v. Wade: The Untold Story of the Landmark Supreme Court Decision That Made Abortion Legal*, New York: MacMillan, 1988.

"The Great Abortion Case (Roe v. Wade)," New York Review of Books, June 29, 1989, Vol. 36, No. 1, pp. 49-53.

Irons, Peter H., *The Courage of Their Convictions*, New York: Free Press, 1988.

Kauper, Paul G., "Penumbras, Peripheries, Emanations, Things Fundamental and Things Forgotten: The Griswold Case," Michigan Law Review 64: 235-258.

Lawson, Don, *Landmark Supreme Court Cases*, Hillside, NJ: Enslow Publishers, Inc., 1987.

Lewis, Anthony, *Gideon's Trumpet*, New York: Random House, 1964.

Morgan, Richard E., *The Supreme Court and Religion*, New York: Free Press, 1972.

Nimmer, Melville B., "The Meaning of Symbolic Speech to the First Amendment," UCLA Law Review 21:29-62.

Rehnquist, William H., *The Supreme Court: How It Was, How It Is*, New York: Morrow, 1987.

Rubin, Eva, *Abortion, Politics, and the Courts: Roe v. Wade and Its Aftermath*, New York: Greenwood Press, 1987.

Schwartz, Bernard, *Behind Bakke: Affirmative Action and the Supreme Court*, New York: New York University Press, 1988.

Schwartz, Bernard, *Super Chief: Earl Warren and His Supreme Court: A Judicial Biography*, New York: New York University Press, 1983.

Schwartz, Herman, ed., *The Burger Years: Rights and Wrongs in the Supreme Court, 1969-1986, New York: Viking, 1987.*

Ungar, Sanford J., *The Papers and The Papers: An Account of the Legal and Political Battle Over the Pentagon Papers*, New York: Dutton, 1972.

Wilkinson, J. Harvie III, *From Brown to Bakke: The Supreme Court and School Integration, 1954-1978*, New York: Oxford University Press, 1979.

Wolters, Raymond, *The Burden of Brown: Thirty Years of School Desegregation*, Knoxville, TN: The University of Tennessee Press, 1984.

Woods, Geraldine, *Affirmative Action*, New York: Impact Books, 1989.

Woodward, Bob, and Scott Armstrong, *The Brethren: Inside the Supreme Court*, New York: Simon & Schuster, 1979.

SUPREME COURT JUSTICES

The following Justices of the Supreme Court participated in the Landmark Decisions reported in this book:

HUGO L. BLACK Associate Justice, 1937-1971
Appointed by Franklin D. Roosevelt

HARRY A. BLACKMUN Associate Justice, 1970-
Appointed by Richard Nixon

WILLIAM J. BRENNAN Associate Justice, 1956-1990
Appointed by Dwight D. Eisenhower

WARREN E. BURGER Chief Justice, 1969-1986
Appointed by Richard Nixon

HAROLD H. BURTON Associate Justice, 1945-1958
Appointed by Harry Truman

THOMAS C. CLARK Associate Justice, 1949-1967
Appointed by Harry Truman

WILLIAM O. DOUGLAS Associate Justice, 1939-1975
Appointed by Franklin D. Roosevelt

FELIX FRANKFURTER Associate Justice, 1939-1962
Appointed by Franklin D. Roosevelt

ARTHUR J. GOLDBERG Associate Justice, 1962-1965
Appointed by John F. Kennedy

JOHN M. HARLAN Associate Justice, 1955-1971
Appointed by Dwight D. Eisenhower

ROBERT H. JACKSON Associate Justice, 1941-1954
Appointed by Franklin D. Roosevelt

ANTHONY M. KENNEDY Associate Justice, 1988-
Appointed by Ronald Reagan

THURGOOD MARSHALL Associate Justice, 1967-
Appointed by Lyndon B. Johnson

SHERMAN MINTON Associate Justice, 1949-1956
Appointed by Harry Truman

SANDRA DAY O'CONNOR Associate Justice, 1981-
Appointed by Ronald Reagan

LEWIS F. POWELL, JR. Associate Justice, 1972-1987
Appointed by Richard Nixon

STANLEY F. REED Associate Justice, 1938-1957
Appointed by Franklin D. Roosevelt

WILLIAM H. REHNQUIST Associate Justice, 1971-1986
Appointed by Richard Nixon
Chief Justice, 1986-
Appointed by Ronald Reagan

ANTONIN SCALIA Associate Justice, 1986-
Appointed by Ronald Reagan

JOHN PAUL STEVENS Associate Justice, 1975-
Appointed by Gerald Ford

POTTER STEWART Associate Justice, 1958-1981
Appointed by Dwight D. Eisenhower

EARL WARREN Chief Justice, 1953-1969
Appointed by Dwight D. Eisenhower

BYRON R. WHITE Associate Justice, 1962-
Appointed by John F. Kennedy

INDEX

Coming Soon in the Landmark Decisions Series

LANDMARK SEXUAL RIGHTS DECISIONS

LANDMARK RELIGIOUS FREEDOM DECISIONS

LANDMARK CIVIL RIGHTS DECISIONS

LANDMARK FREEDOM OF SPEECH DECISIONS

LANDMARK CRIMINAL JUSTICE DECISIONS

LANDMARK DECISIONS OVERRULED

ORDER FORM

Additional copies of LANDMARK DECISIONS OF
THE UNITED STATES SUPREME COURT may be
ordered by sending $14.95 (we pay shipping &
handling) to the address below.

California residents, please add 90 cents sales tax.

Any book may be returned at any time for any reason
and a full refund will be made, no questions asked.

Name: _____

Address: _____

City: _____ **State:** _____ **Zip:** _____

Mail your check or money order to: Excellent
Books, Post Office Box 7121, Beverly Hills, CA
90212-7121